Quick & Easy Cooking

Quick & Easy Cooking

This edition first published in 1989
exclusively for Marks and Spencer p.l.c.
by arrangement with
the Octopus Publishing Group
Michelin House, 81 Fulham Road
London SW3 6RB
© Hennerwood Publications Limited, 1989
ISBN 0 86273 535 1
Typeset by MS Filmsetting Limited, Frome, Somerset
Printed in Spain by Imprenta Hispano-Americana, Barcelona

Contents

Simple soups
◆
& STARTERS

*A three-course menu can be prepared in a very
short time, if you choose recipes that are quick to
make or that can be left to cook or chill while
others are being attended to. The recipes in this
chapter are for first courses, and some of these
take no longer than 10–15 minutes to prepare.*

*There are hot and cold soups, both smooth and
chunky. There are starters based on fruit such as
sweet pears with a creamy Camembert cheese
sauce, and a refreshing cocktail made from
grapefruit and kiwi fruit. Fish starters include a
rich pâté made with prawns and soft cheese,
elegant rolls of smoked trout and salmon filled
with horseradish cream, a piquant salad of pickled
herring, apple and pickled cucumber in soured
cream, and a spicy crab dip to be served hot.
There's also an unusual Chinese starter called
Bang-Bang Chicken.*

LEFT: Hot Crab Dip (see recipe on page 11); RIGHT:
Pears with Camembert Sauce (see recipe on page 8).

PEARS WITH CAMEMBERT SAUCE

4 ripe dessert pears, peeled, cored and sliced
1 tablespoon lemon juice
150ml (¼ pint) soured cream
2 tablespoons double cream
50g (2oz) Camembert cheese, chopped
pinch of cayenne pepper
4 mint sprigs, to garnish

Preparation time: 10 minutes

1. Brush the pears with lemon juice to preserve the colour and arrange them on individual serving plates.
2. Put the soured cream, double cream and Camembert into the bowl of a blender or food processor and blend until smooth.
3. Pour the sauce next to the pears, sprinkle with cayenne and garnish each plate with mint.

Serves 4

Nutrition content per serving   Carbohydrate: 13g Fat: 15g
Fibre: 3g Kilocalories: 196

SMOOTH AVOCADO SOUP

25g (1oz) butter
1 tablespoon finely chopped onion
15g (½oz) plain flour
300ml (½ pint) chicken stock
1 ripe avocado, peeled, stoned and chopped
1–2 teaspoons lemon juice
pinch of finely grated lemon rind
salt
freshly ground black pepper
150ml (¼ pint) creamy milk
TO GARNISH:
4 tablespoons cream
chopped fresh chives

Preparation time: 15 minutes
Cooking time: about 15 minutes

1. Melt the butter in a saucepan. Add the onion and fry until soft but not coloured. Stir in the flour and cook for 1 minute. Gradually stir in the stock and bring to the boil. Simmer for 3–4 minutes.
2. Add the avocado with the lemon juice, rind and salt and pepper to taste. Simmer for 5 minutes, then sieve the soup or purée in a blender or food processor.

3. Return to a clean saucepan and stir in the milk. Reheat without boiling. Adjust the seasoning and pour into soup bowls. Stir in the cream and sprinkle with chives.

Note: This soup can also be served chilled. After sieving or puréeing, add the milk and cream and chill thoroughly.

Serves 2

Nutrition content per serving   Carbohydrate: 13g Fat: 42g
Fibre: 2g Kilocalories: 459

PRAWN & SOFT CHEESE PATE

175g (6oz) full fat soft cheese
3 spring onions or 1 shallot, peeled and very finely chopped
250g (9oz) peeled cooked prawns or shrimps
juice of 1 small lemon
salt
freshly ground black pepper
1½ tablespoons finely chopped fresh dill or fennel
TO GARNISH:
whole cooked prawns
fronds of dill or fennel

Preparation time: 20 minutes

1. In a mixing bowl, beat the cheese with a wooden spoon until it is smooth. Add the onion or shallot.
2. Chop the prawns and stir into the cheese mixture. Add the lemon juice, season well with salt and pepper, then add the herb. Mix well together.
3. Divide the mixture betwen 4 cocottes or small individual dishes. Smooth the tops. Garnish with prawns and dill or fennel fronds.

Serves 4

Nutrition content per serving   Carbohydrate: trace Fat: 22g
Fibre: trace Kilocalories: 261

TOP: Smooth Avocado Soup; BOTTOM: Prawn & Soft Cheese Pâté.

GRAPEFRUIT & KIWI COCKTAILS

3 large or 6 small grapefruit, halved
4–5 kiwi fruit, peeled and thinly sliced
6–8 tablespoons medium sherry or Madeira
4–6 tablespoons demerara sugar
fresh mint sprigs, to garnish

Preparation time: 20 minutes, plus chilling

1. Using a grapefruit knife, carefully remove the segments from each grapefruit half. Discard any pith and cut up the segments.
2. Gently toss the grapefruit pieces with the slices of kiwi fruit and spoon into the grapefruit shells. Sprinkle with the sherry and sugar.
3. Chill in the refrigerator for 1 hour before serving, garnished with mint sprigs.

Serves 6

Nutrition content per serving   Carbohydrate: 24g Fat: 0g
Fibre: 2g Kilocalories: 111

BANG-BANG CHICKEN

This popular dish served in Peking and Sichuan restaurants is extremely simple to cook. If you cannot get sesame sauce (sometimes called sesame paste), an acceptable substitute is peanut butter creamed with a little sesame seed oil.

175g (6oz) chicken breast meat, skinned
1 lettuce heart
SAUCE:
1 tablespoon sesame sauce
1 tablespoon light soy sauce
2 teaspoons vinegar
1 teaspoon chilli sauce
1 teaspoon sugar
2 tablespoons stock
cucumber 'flower', to garnish

Preparation time: 15 minutes
Cooking time: 15 minutes

1. Cover the chicken meat with cold water in a saucepan and bring to the boil, then reduce the heat and simmer gently for 10 minutes. Remove the chicken and beat it with a rolling pin until it is softened (hence the name of the dish).
2. Cut the lettuce leaves into shreds and place them on a serving dish. Pull the chicken meat into shreds with your fingers and place on top of the lettuce leaves.
3. Mix together all the ingredients for the sauce and pour evenly over the chicken. Serve cold, garnished with a cucumber 'flower'.

Serves 4

Nutrition content per serving   Carbohydrate: 2g Fat: 4g
Fibre: 0g Kilocalories: 83

HOT CRAB DIP

175–225g (6–8oz) crab meat (white and brown mixed)
2 tablespoons lemon juice
250ml (8fl oz) soured cream
50g (2oz) mayonnaise
½–1 teaspoon Worcestershire sauce
dash of Tabasco sauce (optional)

Preparation time: about 5 minutes
Cooking time: 2 minutes

1. If using frozen or canned crabmeat, drain it well. Mix all the ingredients, except the parsley or chives, in a saucepan and heat slowly over a low flame.
2. Tip the mixture into a heated bowl and stand on a candle-warmer or electric hotplate. Sprinkle with the parsley or chives. Serve with savoury biscuits, crisps and vegetables for dipping.

Serves 6–8

Nutrition content per serving   Carbohydrate: 2–1g Fat: 16–12g
Fibre: 0g Kilocalories: 181–135

TOP: Grapefruit & Kiwi Cocktails; BOTTOM: Bang-Bang Chicken.

PARMA HAM WITH AVOCADO

1 ripe avocado
6 slices Parma ham, about 75g (3oz) total
DRESSING:
1 tablespoon olive oil
1 teaspoon lemon juice
1 garlic clove, peeled and crushed
2 teaspoons chopped fresh parsley
salt
freshly ground black pepper

Preparation time: 10 minutes

1. Cut the avocado in half and remove the stone. Peel off the skin and cut each half lengthways into thin slices.
2. Arrange the avocado and ham on a serving dish.
3. Place all the dressing ingredients in a screw-topped jar and shake well to mix.
4. Pour the dressing over the avocado and serve immediately.

Variation: Parma ham with figs: Serve 2 ripe figs per person, cutting each down through the centre in a cross. Open out the figs and arrange on the plates with the slices of Parma ham. Omit the dressing.

Serves 2

Nutrition content per serving   Carbohydrate: 2g Fat: 35g
Fibre: 2g Kilocalories: 378

LEMON CHICKEN SOUP

25g (1oz) butter
1 medium onion, peeled and chopped
750ml (1¼ pints) chicken stock
100g (4oz) cooked chicken or turkey meat,
  roughly chopped
1 tablespoon cornflour
3 tablespoons lemon juice
½ teaspoon salt
white pepper
150ml (¼ pint) double cream
2 egg yolks
TO GARNISH:
chopped fresh chervil or parsley
shredded lemon rind

Preparation time: 15 minutes
Cooking time: about 15 minutes

1. Melt the butter in a large pan, add the onion and cook over a low heat for about 10 minutes until the onion is soft and translucent.
2. Place the onion, stock and cooked chicken in a blender or food processor and add the cornflour. Blend until smooth. Return to the pan and bring to the boil, stirring. Stir in the lemon juice, salt and pepper. Finally add the cream. Cool slightly.
3. Mix a little of the soup with the egg yolks and add to the pan, stirring continuously. Do not allow to boil or the egg yolks will curdle. Serve immediately, with chopped chervil or parsley and lemon rind sprinkled on top.

Serves 4–6

Nutrition content per serving   Carbohydrate: 5–3g Fat: 29–19g
Fibre: 0g Kilocalories: 313–209

POTTED SMOKED HADDOCK

350g (12oz) smoked haddock fillet, flaked
pinch of grated nutmeg
150ml (¼ pint) single cream
salt
freshly ground black pepper
50g (2oz) butter

Preparation time: 10 minutes
Cooking time: 12–15 minutes
Oven: 200°C, 400°F, Gas Mark 6

1. Mix the flaked fish with the nutmeg, cream, and salt and pepper to taste. Spoon the mixture into 4 cocottes or small ovenproof dishes. Dot the surfaces with small knobs of the butter.
2. Stand the dishes in a roasting tin and add sufficient boiling water to come halfway up the sides of the dishes. Bake in a preheated oven for 12–15 minutes until golden. Serve at once.

Serves 4

Nutrition content per serving   Carbohydrate: 1g Fat: 19g
Fibre: 0g Kilocalories: 262

LEFT: Lemon Chicken Soup; RIGHT: Parma Ham with Avocado; BOTTOM: Potted Smoked Haddock.

QUICK GAZPACHO

This soup keeps well in the refrigerator in a covered bowl for 2–3 days. It does not freeze.

2 tablespoons lemon juice
2 teaspoons wine vinegar
½ teaspoon Worcestershire sauce
600ml (1 pint) tomato juice
1–2 garlic cloves, peeled and crushed
3 large tomatoes, skinned and finely chopped
5cm (2 inch) piece cucumber, grated or chopped
1–2 tablespoons finely grated onion
½ green pepper, cored, seeded and finely chopped
salt
freshly ground black pepper
few ice cubes (optional)
TO GARNISH:
fresh basil sprigs or chopped fresh herbs
diced cucumber, pepper and tomato

Preparation time: 30 minutes, plus chilling

1. Put the lemon juice, wine vinegar and Worcestershire sauce into a bowl and add the tomato juice and garlic. Mix well.
2. Stir in the tomatoes, cucumber, onion and green pepper and mix well. If a smooth soup is preferred, purée in a blender or food processor. Season to taste. Cover the bowl tightly and chill thoroughly.
3. To serve, pour into a bowl over 2–3 ice cubes, if liked, and garnish with basil. Serve the diced vegetables separately to sprinkle over the soup.

Serves 2

Nutrition content per serving   Carbohydrate: 18g Fat: 0g
Fibre: 3g Kilocalories: 86

SMOKED TROUT & SALMON ROLLS

Red caviar is not strictly caviar at all since it comes from the dog salmon, native to Siberian rivers running into the Pacific, and off the west Canadian coast. The taste is similar but more salty that the true caviar, which would be wasted in this dish as its delicate flavour would be lost. Red lumpfish roe makes an excellent substitute and is more widely available.

1 smoked trout, about 350–400g (12–14oz), skinned and filleted into 4 long pieces
6 tablespoons double cream
4 tablespoons soured cream
1½ tablespoons creamed horseradish
¼ teaspoon cayenne pepper
12 thin slices smoked salmon, about 425g (15oz) total weight
50g (2oz) red caviar or red lumpfish roe
freshly ground black pepper
fresh chives
12 thin slices of lemon
fresh dill sprigs, to garnish

Preparation time: 40 minutes, plus chilling

1. Cut each fillet of smoked trout into 3 pieces and reserve.
2. Beat the double cream until it forms soft peaks, then fold in the soured cream and creamed horseradish. Season with the cayenne pepper and then spread each slice of smoked salmon with a little of the mixture.
3. Put a small piece of caviar or lumpfish roe at one end of each slice, spreading it slightly, then sprinkle with pepper.
4. Place a piece of smoked trout on top of the caviar, then carefully roll up the salmon slice, starting at the smoked trout end. Tie with chives.
5. Arrange the rolls on a platter and garnish with twisted lemon slices and sprigs of dill. Cover and chill for at least 1 hour.
6. Serve chilled with lightly buttered brown bread.

Serves 6

Nutrition content per serving   Carbohydrate: 1g Fat: 16g
Fibre: 0g Kilocalories: 285

TOP: Quick Gazpacho; BOTTOM: Smoked Trout & Salmon Rolls.

CRAB & BACON OLIVES

175g (6oz) crab meat
1 small egg, beaten
75g (3oz) soft breadcrumbs
120ml (4fl oz) tomato juice
1 teaspoon chopped fresh basil
1 teaspoon chopped fresh parsley
salt
freshly ground black pepper
12 back bacon rashers, rinds removed
TO GARNISH:
tomato wedges
fresh parsley sprigs

Preparation time: 20 minutes
Cooking time: 5–10 minutes

1. Mix together the crab meat, egg, breadcrumbs and enough of the tomato juice to bind. Add the basil, parsley and salt and pepper to taste. Mix well together and shape into 12 fingers.
2. Wrap a bacon rasher round each crab finger, then secure with a wooden cocktail stick.
3. Place on a rack under a preheated grill and cook until the bacon is crisp, turning frequently.
4. Arrange on a hot dish and garnish with the tomatoes and parsley sprigs.

Serves 4

Nutrition content per serving   Carbohydrate: 10g Fat: 40g
Fibre: 1g Kilocalories: 494

GREEN PEA SOUP

25g (1oz) bacon fat
3 large spring onions, chopped
outside leaves of a lettuce, roughly shredded
450g (1lb) frozen peas
1 litre (1¾ pints) stock or water
salt
freshly ground black pepper
3 tablespoons double cream

Preparation time: 15 minutes
Cooking time: about 10 minutes

1. Melt the bacon fat in a pan, add the spring onions and lettuce leaves and cook for 2 minutes. Add the peas, stock and seasoning, bring to the boil and simmer for 5 minutes.
2. Sieve or purée in a blender or food processor. Return to the pan and reheat gently. Taste and adjust the seasoning, stir in the cream and pour into bowls. If liked, garnish with croûtons.

Serves 4

Nutrition content per serving   Carbohydrate: 9g Fat: 7g
Fibre: 9g Kilocalories: 119

PICKLED HERRING SALAD

1 × 340ml (12fl oz) jar pickled herrings, drained
3 pickled dill cucumbers, thinly sliced
2 red-skinned dessert apples, cored and sliced
1 bunch spring onions, trimmed and chopped
150ml (¼ pint) soured cream
1 tablespoon chopped fresh dill, or ½ teaspoon dried
   dill
chopped spring onions, to garnish

Preparation time: 20 minutes

1. Cut the herrings into thin strips and place in a bowl. Add the sliced dill cucumbers, apples, spring onions, soured cream and dill and toss well to mix.
2. Spoon into a chilled serving dish, sprinkle with chopped spring onions and serve.

Serves 4

Nutrition content per serving   Carbohydrate: 12g Fat: 21g
Fibre: 2g Kilocalories: 290

LEFT: Green Pea Soup; RIGHT: Crab & Bacon Olives; BOTTOM: Pickled Herring Salad.

Family meals

◆

Busy cooks are always looking for new ideas for main dishes that are quick to prepare but are still appetizing and nourishing. The recipes in this chapter will suggest lots of ways to vary everyday menus.

Minced beef is always a popular choice for family meals as it is versatile and very economical. Here you will find it combined with a savoury tomato sauce and green noodles in a casserole, as well as mixed with apple, raisins and olives for a Spanish flavour.

There are lamb, kidney and sausage kebabs, and Chinese-style lamb stir-fried with spring onions. Chunks of tender pork are cooked with apricots, and grilled bacon chops are topped with a spicy-sweet plum sauce. Chicken is cooked in a sweet-sour sauce with pineapple, and coated with crisps and cheese for oven baking. If you fancy fish, there are grilled cod steaks with a Cheddar and peanut topping, prawns in a creamy sherry sauce, and kebabs of smoked mackerel with oranges.

Pork Fillet with Apricots (see recipe on page 20).

PORK FILLET WITH APRICOTS

450g (1lb) pork fillet, cut into bite-size pieces
2 tablespoons seasoned flour
50g (2oz) butter
1 × 400g (14oz) can apricot halves
2 tablespoons Worcestershire sauce
2 tablespoons demerara sugar
2 teaspoons vinegar
2 teaspoons lemon juice
120ml (4fl oz) water

Preparation time: 15 minutes
Cooking time: 20 minutes

1. Toss the pork pieces in seasoned flour. Heat the butter in a frying pan and fry the pork until lightly browned.
2. Drain the apricots, reserving juice, and chop all but 3 halves. Mix 120ml (4fl oz) juice with the remaining ingredients.
3. Add any remaining seasoned flour to the pork and pour in the apricot sauce and chopped fruit. Bring to the boil, stirring. Reduce the heat, cover and simmer for 15 minutes.
4. Spoon the pork and sauce on to a serving dish. Garnish with the remaining apricot halves.

Serves 4

Nutrition content per serving   Carbohydrate: 87g Fat: 19g
Fibre: 3g Kilocalories: 612

DEEP-FRIED CURRIED POUSSINS

50g (2oz) butter
50g (2oz) plain flour
2 teaspoons curry powder
150ml ($\frac{1}{4}$ pint) chicken stock
1 egg
2 × 450g (1lb) poussins, skinned and jointed
salt
dry breadcrumbs
oil for deep frying
lemon wedges and parsley sprig, to garnish

Preparation time: 20 minutes
Cooking time: about 10 minutes

1. Melt the butter in a saucepan and stir in the flour and curry powder. Cook for 1 minute, then gradually stir in the stock. Bring to the boil, stirring, and simmer until thickened. Cool slightly, then beat in the egg.
2. Season the poussins with salt, then coat first with the sauce and then with the breadcrumbs.
3. Deep fry in oil heated to 185°C (360°F) for 5–7 minutes or until golden brown. Drain on paper towels, garnish and serve hot.

Serves 4

Nutrition content per serving   Carbohydrate: 15g Fat: 36g
Fibre: 1g Kilocalories: 500

PORK CHOW MEIN

225g (8oz) egg noodles
275g (10oz) pork fillet
3 teaspoons cornflour
100g (4oz) bamboo shoots
100g (4oz) spinach leaves
$\frac{1}{4}$ cucumber
5 tablespoons oil
2 tablespoons soy sauce
1 tablespoon dry sherry
1 teaspoon salt
1 teaspoon sugar
1 teaspoon sesame seed oil, to garnish

Preparation time: 20–25 minutes
Cooking time: 6–8 minutes

1. Cook the noodles in boiling water for 5 minutes until soft but not sticky. Drain in a sieve and rinse with cold water.
2. Cut the pork into shreds the size of a matchstick and mix them with 2 teaspoons cornflour. Cut the bamboo shoots, spinach and cucumber into thin shreds the same size as the pork.
3. Heat about half the oil in a wok or frying pan. Place the noodles in a large bowl and pour over the hot oil. Stir to coat the noodles evenly. Tip them into the wok or pan and stir-fry for 2–3 minutes. Remove with a slotted spoon to a warmed serving dish.
4. Heat the remaining oil in the pan and stir-fry the bamboo shoots, cucumber, spinach and pork. Mix together the remaining ingredients and pour into the pan. Cook for about 2 minutes, then pour the mixture over the noodles, garnish with sesame seed oil and serve.

Serves 4

Nutrition content per serving   Carbohydrate: 46g Fat: 30g
Fibre: 3g Kilocalories: 536

TOP: Deep-Fried Curried Poussins; BOTTOM: Pork Chow Mein.

BEEF NOODLE CASSEROLE

175g (6oz) green noodles
750g (1½lb) minced beef
2 onions, peeled and chopped
1–2 garlic cloves, peeled and crushed
2 teaspoons cornflour
1 × 425g (15oz) can tomatoes
150ml (¼ pint) beef stock
1 tablespoon soy sauce
1 tablespoon Worcestershire sauce
1 tablespoon tomato purée
1 teaspoon dried oregano
salt
freshly ground black pepper
25g (1oz) butter
25g (1oz) plain flour
300ml (½ pint) milk
40–50g (1½–2oz) mature Cheddar cheese, grated
fresh bay leaves, to garnish

Preparation time: 20 minutes
Cooking time: 25–30 minutes
Oven: 200°C, 400°F, Gas Mark 6

1. Cook the noodles in boiling salted water for 6–7 minutes until partly cooked. Drain.
2. Cook the minced beef gently in a pan with no extra fat until browned and crumbly, stirring frequently. Add the onions and garlic and continue cooking for 3–4 minutes.
3. Blend the cornflour with some of the juice from the tomatoes, then stir into the beef with the tomatoes, stock, soy sauce, Worcestershire sauce, tomato purée, oregano, and salt and pepper to taste. Bring to the boil and cook for 2 minutes.
4. Put half the noodles in the base of a casserole, cover with the meat mixture, then add the rest of the noodles.
5. Melt the butter in a pan, stir in the flour and cook for 1 minute, then gradually add the milk and bring to the boil for 1 minute. Add salt and pepper to taste and pour over the noodles.
6. Sprinkle over the cheese. Cover and cook in a preheated oven for 15 minutes, then uncover and continue cooking for a further 10–15 minutes or until the topping is brown and crispy. Serve hot, garnished with fresh bay leaves.

Serves 4–5

Nutrition content per serving   Carbohydrate: 50–40g
Fat: 45–36g Fibre: 4–3g Kilocalories: 789–631

SWEET & SOUR CHICKEN

25g (1oz) butter
4 boned chicken breasts, skinned and thinly sliced
1 × 225g (8oz) can sliced pineapple
1 green pepper, cored, seeded and cut into strips
1 tablespoon brown sugar
1 tablespoon vinegar
2 tablespoons soy sauce
1 tablespoon cornflour
100g (4oz) button mushrooms, halved
salt
freshly ground black pepper

Preparation time: 20 minutes
Cooking time: about 35 minutes

1. Melt the butter in a large frying pan, add the chicken and fry over brisk heat until lightly coloured.
2. Drain the pineapple and make up the juice to 200ml (7fl oz) with water. Chop the pineapple slices roughly. Stir the green pepper, sugar, vinegar and soy sauce into the pineapple juice and add to the pan. Bring to the boil, stirring constantly.
3. Lower the heat, cover and simmer for 15–20 minutes or until the chicken is tender.
4. Mix the cornflour to a paste with a little water. Add to the pan and stir in well, then cook until the sauce thickens, stirring constantly. Add the chopped pineapple and the mushrooms and heat through for 5 minutes. Taste and adjust seasoning, and serve hot.

Serves 4

Nutrition content per serving   Carbohydrate: 18g Fat: 8g
Fibre: 1g Kilocalories: 222

TOP: Beef Noodle Casserole; BOTTOM: Sweet & Sour Chicken.

HAKE IN PARSLEY SAUCE

550g (1¼lb) hake, skinned and cut into 2.5cm
    (1 inch) slices
1 teaspoon mild curry powder
50g (2oz) parsley sprigs
150ml (¼ pint) fish stock
1 tablespoon dry sherry
1 teaspoon lemon juice
salt
freshly ground black pepper
TO GARNISH:
dill sprigs
lemon slices

Preparation time: 15 minutes
Cooking time: 15 minutes

1. Wipe and dry the hake slices. Sprinkle them
with the curry powder.
2. Heat a non-stick frying pan and fry the fish
over moderate heat for about 8 minutes, turning
each slice once. Remove the fish and keep it
warm.
3. Add the parsley, fish stock, sherry and lemon
juice to the pan and season with salt and pepper.
Bring the sauce to the boil and boil for 2
minutes. Purée the sauce in a blender. Taste and
adjust the seasoning if necessary.
4. Pour the sauce on to a heated serving dish,
arrange the fish on top and garnish with sprigs
of dill and lemon slices.

Serves 4

Nutrition content per serving   Carbohydrate: trace Fat: 1g
Fibre: 1g Kilocalories: 110

ABOVE: Hake in Parsley Sauce.
RIGHT: Bacon Chops with Plum Sauce (top); Spanish
Mince (bottom).

BACON CHOPS WITH PLUM SAUCE

2 lean bacon chops, about 2.5cm (1 inch) thick,
    rind and excess fat removed
75g (3oz) plum jam
2 tablespoons wine vinegar
2 tablespoons water
1 teaspoon dry mustard
salt
freshly ground black pepper
large pinch of dried mixed herbs

Preparation time: 5 minutes
Cooking time: 10–15 minutes

1. Grill the chops under a preheated moderate
grill for 4–5 minutes on each side.
2. Meanwhile, put all the remaining ingredients
with salt and pepper to taste into a small pan
and bring to the boil gently, stirring. Simmer
for 2 minutes.
3. Serve the sauce spooned over the chops.

Serves 2

Nutrition content per serving   Carbohydrate: 26g Fat: 9g
Fibre: trace Kilocalories: 271

SPANISH MINCE

1 medium onion, peeled and thinly sliced
2 tablespoons oil
2 garlic cloves, peeled and crushed
550g (1¼lb) minced beef
2 dessert apples, cored and grated
50g (2oz) raisins
300 ml (½ pint) beef stock
75g (3oz) stuffed olives, thickly sliced
coarsely grated rind of 1 orange
salt
freshly ground black pepper

Preparation time: 10 minutes
Cooking time: 40 minutes

1. Fry the onion in the oil in a frying pan for 2
minutes. Add the garlic and mince and cook
until browned. Stir in the apple, raisins and
stock. Cover and simmer for 20 minutes.
2. Stir in the olives, orange rind, salt and
pepper. Simmer for a further 10 minutes.

Serves 4

Nutrition content per serving   Carbohydrate: 18g Fat: 32g
Fibre: 3g Kilocalories: 464

MIXED GRILL ON A SKEWER

225g (8oz) boned leg of lamb, cut into 2.5cm
*   (1 inch) cubes*
4 lambs' kidneys, skinned, cored and quartered
12 small cocktail sausages
12 even-sized button mushrooms
1 green pepper, or ½ red and ½ green, cored, seeded
*   and cut into squares*
BASTE:
1 tablespoon Worcestershire sauce
3 tablespoons tomato chutney
2 tablespoons oil
1 garlic clove, peeled and crushed
juice of ½ lemon
salt
freshly ground black pepper

Preparation time: about 10 minutes
Cooking time: about 10 minutes

1. Thread the lamb, kidneys, cocktail sausages, mushrooms and pepper alternately on to 4 long kebab skewers.
2. Mix together the baste ingredients.
3. Put the kebabs on the rack of the grill pan. Brush or spread half the well-flavoured baste over the kebabs. Place under a preheated moderately hot grill and cook for 5 minutes.
4. Turn the kebabs over and brush with more baste. Cook for a further 5 minutes until the meats are tender.

Serves 4

Nutrition content per serving   Carbohydrate: 11g Fat: 33g
Fibre: 2g Kilocalories: 474

PRAWNS NEWBURG

25g (1oz) butter
100–175g (4–6oz) peeled cooked prawns
3 tablespoons Madeira or sweet sherry
salt
freshly ground black pepper
paprika
1 egg yolk
4 tablespoons single cream
100g (4oz) long-grain rice, freshly cooked
1 tablespoon chopped fresh parsley
fresh parsley sprigs, to garnish

Preparation time: 5 minutes
Cooking time: about 15 minutes

1. Melt the butter in a saucepan. Add the prawns and fry gently for 3–4 minutes. Stir in the Madeira or sherry and simmer gently for a further 3–4 minutes or until slightly reduced. Season well with salt, pepper and paprika.
2. Beat the egg yolk into the cream and whisk gradually into the prawn mixture. Heat gently without boiling until slightly thickened, and adjust the seasoning.
3. Mix the rice and parsley and spoon on to two plates. Spoon the prawn mixture on top and garnish with parsley.

Serves 2

Nutrition content per serving   Carbohydrate: 46g Fat: 22g
Fibre: 2g Kilocalories: 486

LEFT: Mixed Grill on a Skewer.
ABOVE: Prawns Newburg.

TURKEY ESCALOPES WITH CRANBERRY

This is a simple, quick dish to make using either leftover slices of roast turkey breast or the ready-trimmed turkey escalopes now available.

25g (1oz) butter
8 thick slices of roast turkey breast, or 4 fresh
*   turkey escalopes, beaten*
225g (8oz) button mushrooms, sliced
4 tablespoons whole-berry cranberry sauce
a little chicken stock
salt
freshly ground black pepper

Preparation time: 10 minutes
Cooking time: about 15 minutes

1. Melt the butter in a large frying pan. Add the turkey and fry gently for a few minutes on both sides. If using fresh turkey escalopes they will take about 5 minutes on each side before they are tender, depending on thickness.
2. Add the mushrooms to the pan and fry for 1–2 minutes, then stir in the cranberry sauce and a few spoonfuls of chicken stock to make a thin sauce. Season to taste with salt and pepper and transfer to a hot serving platter.

Serves 4

Nutrition content per serving   Carbohydrate: 11g Fat: 8g
Fibre: 1g Kilocalories: 214

COD STEAKS WITH NUTTY TOPPING

Try to buy cod steaks that are cut from near the tail end of the fish with flesh all round the bone.

4 cod steaks
50g (2oz) softened butter
100g (4oz) Cheddar cheese, grated
50g (2oz) salted peanuts, chopped
2 teaspoons milk
watercress, to garnish

Preparation time: 10 minutes
Cooking time: about 20 minutes
Oven: 180°C, 350°F, Gas Mark 4

1. Put the cod steaks in a buttered grill pan and seal under a preheated medium grill for 5 minutes. Turn the steaks over.
2. Blend together the rest of the ingredients and spread on top of each steak.
3. Grill gently for a further 12–15 minutes or until the fish will flake easily when tested with a fork, and the cheese topping is lightly browned. Garnish with watercress and serve.

Serves 4

Nutrition content per serving   Carbohydrate: 1g Fat: 22g
Fibre: 1g Kilocalories: 345

SAUTEED SPICED LAMB

550g (1¼lb) lamb fillet
50g (2oz) butter
1 medium onion, peeled and finely chopped
1 garlic clove, peeled and crushed
½ teaspoon ground cinnamon
2 teaspoons cornflour
150ml (¼ pint) chicken stock
150ml (¼ pint) soured cream
1 tablespoon chopped fresh mint
salt
freshly ground black pepper
chopped fresh mint, to garnish

Preparation time: 5 minutes
Cooking time: about 15 minutes

1. Cut the lamb fillet into thin slices about 5mm (¼ inch) thick.
2. Heat the butter in a frying pan. Add the onion, garlic and cinnamon and fry gently until the onion softens.
3. Add the slices of lamb fillet and cook steadily, turning occasionally, until the lamb is coloured on all sides.
4. Blend the cornflour with the stock and soured cream and add to the pan. Stir until the sauce thickens slightly. Add the mint and salt and pepper to taste, and simmer gently for 8–10 minutes, until the lamb is tender. Serve hot, sprinkled with mint, with noodles.

Serves 4

Nutrition content per serving   Carbohydrate: 4g Fat: 30g
Fibre: 0g Kilocalories: 409

CLOCKWISE FROM THE TOP: Turkey Escalopes with Cranberry; Cod Steaks with Nutty Topping; Sautéed Spiced Lamb.

STIR-FRIED LAMB WITH SPRING ONIONS

This dish must be cooked over the highest heat in the shortest possible time, otherwise the meat will not be tender and juicy.

225–275g (8–10oz) boned leg of lamb
about 12 spring onions
4 tablespoons oil
1 tablespoon soy sauce
½ teaspoon salt
1 tablespoon rice wine or dry sherry
½ teaspoon freshly ground Sichuan or black pepper
2 teaspoons cornflour
1 garlic clove, peeled and crushed
1 tablespoon sesame seed oil
1 tablespoon vinegar
spring onion tassel, to garnish

Preparation time: 15–20 minutes
Cooking time: 4–5 minutes

1. Trim off all the fat from the lamb and cut it into slices as thin as possible. Cut the spring onions in half lengthways, then slice them diagonally.
2. Mix together 1 tablespoon of the oil, the soy sauce, salt, wine or sherry, pepper and cornflour. Add the lamb and spring onions and stir to coat.
3. Heat the remaining oil in a preheated wok or frying pan until smoking. Add the crushed garlic to flavour the oil, followed by the lamb and spring onion mixture. Stir-fry over a high heat for a few seconds, then stir in the sesame seed oil and vinegar. Blend well, and serve hot, garnished with a spring onion tassel.

Serves 4

Nutrition content per serving   Carbohydrate: 3g Fat: 24g
Fibre: 0g Kilocalories: 288

OVEN-BAKED CHICKEN

Quick and simple to prepare, this is an ideal dish for the family as everyone will love its crisp, crunchy topping.

50g (2oz) butter
4 chicken portions, skinned
1 × 70g (2½oz) packet plain crisps, crushed
100g (4oz) cheese, preferably Parmesan or Cheddar, grated
1 tablespoon chopped fresh parsley
¼ teaspoon garlic powder
1 teaspoon chopped fresh tarragon, or ½ teaspoon dried tarragon
salt
freshly ground black pepper

Preparation time: 10 minutes
Cooking time: 45 minutes
Oven: 180°C, 350°F, Gas Mark 4

1. Melt the butter and brush half over the chicken. Mix the crisps together with the remaining ingredients and season to taste. Press this mixture around the chicken portions and put in a casserole. Sprinkle over the remaining melted butter.
2. Bake in a preheated oven for 45 minutes until the chicken is tender and the juices run clear when it is pierced with a skewer. Serve hot.

Serves 4

Nutrition content per serving   Carbohydrate: 9g Fat: 23g
Fibre: 2g Kilocalories: 345

TOP: Stir-Fried Lamb with Spring Onions; BOTTOM: Oven-Baked Chicken.

SEAFOOD CASSEROLE

Choose 2 or 3 types of fish for this recipe, including one firm white fish and one shellfish.

2 tablespoons olive oil
1 garlic clove, peeled and crushed
1 medium onion, peeled and chopped
1 small red pepper, cored, seeded and chopped
450g (1lb) mixed seafood, such as red mullet, scampi, prawns, cod, hake, sole, cut into pieces or steaks
2 tomatoes, skinned and sliced
150ml (¼ pint) white wine
50g (2oz) button mushrooms
salt
freshly ground black pepper
TO GARNISH:
whole cooked prawns
fresh chervil sprigs

Preparation time: 10 minutes
Cooking time: 20–25 minutes

1. Heat the oil in a medium saucepan, add the garlic and onion and fry gently for about 5 minutes.
2. Add the red pepper and cook for 2 minutes. Add the fish and stir to coat in oil.
3. Add the tomatoes, wine, mushrooms, salt and pepper. Bring to the boil, then simmer uncovered for 15–20 minutes until the fish is tender. Garnish and serve.

Serves 2

Nutrition content per serving   Carbohydrate: 7g Fat: 17g
Fibre: 2g Kilocalories: 389

SMOKED MACKEREL & ORANGE KEBABS

225g (8oz) long-grain rice, freshly cooked
15g (½oz) butter
juice and grated rind of ½ orange
4 medium smoked mackerel fillets, skinned
1 teaspoon lemon juice
freshly ground black pepper
3 large oranges, peeled, sliced crossways and slices halved
2 tablespoons blanched almonds

FROM TOP TO BOTTOM: Seafood Casserole; Smoked Mackerel & Orange Kebabs; Liver Stroganoff.

Preparation time: 15 minutes
Cooking time: 5 minutes

1. Mix the hot rice with the butter, orange juice and orange rind. Keep the rice warm.
2. Cut the mackerel fillets across into 2.5cm (1 inch) strips and toss them in the lemon juice. Sprinkle with pepper. Thread the mackerel strips and orange segments alternately on to 4 skewers. Grill under a preheated hot grill for 5 minutes, turning the skewers once.
3. Meanwhile, scatter the almonds on a clean baking sheet and toast them for 2 minutes, turning them once.
4. Just before serving, stir the toasted almonds into the rice. Serve the skewers on the rice.

Serves 4

Nutrition content per serving   Carbohydrate: 58g Fat: 22g
Fibre: 4g Kilocalories: 441

LIVER STROGANOFF

25g (1oz) butter
1 onion, peeled and finely chopped
450g (1lb) lamb's liver, sliced into very thin strips
1 tablespoon tomato purée
1 tablespoon Worcestershire sauce
juice of 1 lemon
225g (8oz) button mushrooms, finely sliced
salt
freshly ground black pepper
150ml (¼ pint) soured cream
finely chopped fresh parsley, to garnish

Preparation time: 15 minutes
Cooking time: 15 minutes

1. Melt the butter in a pan, add the onion and fry over gentle heat until soft. Add the liver and fry for 5 minutes, stirring constantly.
2. Stir in the remaining ingredients except the soured cream, then cook for a further 5 minutes, stirring occasionally.
3. Remove from the heat and stir in the cream, then return the pan to a low heat and warm through without boiling. Taste and adjust the seasoning and serve, sprinkled with parsley.

Serves 4

Nutrition content per serving   Carbohydrate: 6g Fat: 25g
Fibre: 2g Kilocalories: 346

Entertaining

◆

A busy life need not prevent you from entertaining your friends – it isn't necessary to spend hours preparing an elaborate menu because your guests will be just as impressed by dishes put together quickly, but with care.

In this chapter, you'll find lots of ideas for easy yet special main dishes, and none of them takes longer than 45 minutes to make. Lamb steaks cut from the leg are grilled and then topped with pats of lemon and parsley butter. Rounds of pork fillet are cooked with orange juice and ginger marmalade. Succulent fillet steaks are given a caramelized mustard topping and served with a brandy sauce. Cubes of monkfish are flavoured with cumin and mint and then grilled on skewers. Salmon steaks are served with a buttery red wine sauce. Pieces of turkey breast are topped with mushrooms and mozzarella cheese and finished under the grill.

Scallop & Bacon Kebabs (see recipe on page 36).

SCALLOP & BACON KEBABS

The tender meat of the scallop is perfectly complemented by the flavour of bacon.

8 large or 16 small scallops
8 unsmoked streaky bacon rashers, rinds removed
1 egg, beaten
2 tablespoons fine white breadcrumbs
25g (1oz) butter, melted
lemon wedges, to serve

Preparation time: 25 minutes
Cooking time: 10–15 minutes

1. Wash the scallops and cut out any black threads. Take off the coral and cut the white meat of large scallops in half.
2. Stretch the bacon rashers with the back of a knife and cut each rasher in half. Wrap a piece of bacon around each piece of white scallop meat.
3. Dip the coral pieces into the egg and coat evenly with breadcrumbs. Brush carefully with melted butter.
4. Arrange the pieces of scallop on skewers, alternating the bacon-wrapped white meat and the breadcrumbed coral.
5. Place under a preheated moderately hot grill or over a barbecue and cook for 10–15 minutes, turning occasionally, until the fish is cooked and golden brown.
6. Serve with lemon wedges or, if liked, with lemony melted butter.

Serves 4

Nutrition content per serving   Carbohydrate: 3g Fat: 30g
Fibre: trace Kilocalories: 429

VEAL WITH VERMOUTH & ORANGE

4 veal escalopes, weighing about 100g (4oz) each
2 tablespoons plain flour
salt
freshly ground black pepper
50g (2oz) butter
2 tablespoons olive oil
juice of 2 oranges
150ml ($\frac{1}{4}$ pint) dry white vermouth
2 teaspoons dark soft brown sugar
TO GARNISH:
1–2 oranges, peeled and segmented
fresh chervil sprig

Preparation time: 10 minutes
Cooking time: about 25 minutes

1. Beat the escalopes with a mallet or rolling pin to make them very thin. Pat them dry with paper towels, then coat evenly in the flour seasoned with salt and pepper.
2. Melt 25g (1oz) butter with the oil in a large heavy-based frying pan. Add the escalopes and fry over moderate heat for about 3 minutes on each side until lightly browned.
3. Measure the orange juice and make up to 150ml ($\frac{1}{4}$ pint) with water, if necessary. Pour over the escalopes, then simmer gently for about 8 minutes or until the veal is tender, turning it over once during this time.
4. Remove the veal from the pan with a slotted spoon, arrange on a warmed serving platter and keep hot in a very low oven.
5. Pour the vermouth into the pan, stir in the sugar and increase the heat. Boil vigorously until the sauce has thickened and reduced, stirring continuously with a wooden spoon to loosen any sediment from the bottom and sides of the pan.
6. Remove the pan from the heat, stir in the remaining butter in pieces, then whisk until the butter has dissolved and the sauce has a shiny glaze. Taste and adjust the seasoning, then pour over the veal. Garnish with orange segments and a chervil sprig, and serve immediately.

Serves 4

Nutrition content per serving   Carbohydrate: 15g Fat: 21g
Fibre: 1g Kilocalories: 366

Veal with Vermouth & Orange.

MONKFISH KEBABS WITH CUMIN & MINT

Cumin is a taste that once acquired is never lost. Combined with the sweetness of mint, it gives monkfish an exotic flavour.

1.5kg (3lb) tailpiece monkfish, skinned and
*   filleted*
120ml (4fl oz) olive oil
1 tablespoon lemon juice
1 tablespoon cumin seeds, lightly crushed
2 tablespoons finely chopped fresh mint, lightly
*   pounded, or 1 tablespoon dried mint*
salt
freshly ground black pepper
fresh mint sprigs, to garnish
150ml (¼ pint) plain unsweetened yogurt, chilled,
*   to serve*

Preparation time: 10 minutes, plus marinating
Cooking time: 5 minutes

1. Cut the monkfish into bite-sized cubes and put into a large shallow dish. Combine the oil, lemon juice, cumin seeds and mint. Season with salt and a fair amount of black pepper then pour over the fish. Stir to coat, then leave at room temperature to marinate for 1 hour.
2. Thread the fish on to 6 skewers and cook under a preheated hot grill for 4–5 minutes, turning every minute until just done, brushing frequently with the marinade.
3. Serve immediately garnished with mint sprigs, providing the yogurt as a dip, with pitta or crusty bread.

Serves 6

Nutrition content per serving   Carbohydrate: 2g Fat: 3g
Fibre: trace Kilocalories: 307

PORK MEDALLIONS WITH GINGER

25g (1oz) butter
450g (1lb) pork fillet, sliced into 1cm (½ inch)
*   thick rounds or medallions*
salt
freshly ground black pepper
1 tablespoon ginger marmalade
1 tablespoon brown sugar
1 tablespoon orange juice
1 tablespoon cider vinegar
4 spring onions, trimmed and finely shredded
julienne strips of orange rind, to garnish

Preparation time: 15 minutes
Cooking time: 10–12 minutes

1. Melt the butter in a frying pan. Add the pork and salt and pepper to taste. Cook for about 6–8 minutes until golden and tender on both sides. Remove with a slotted spoon and arrange decoratively on a warmed serving plate. Keep warm.
2. Add the marmalade, sugar, orange juice, cider vinegar and spring onions to the pan juices. Heat until the mixture forms a syrupy glaze.
3. Spoon over the pork medallions and garnish with julienne strips of orange rind.

Variation: Medallions of pork can also be cooked with apricots and cinnamon. Add 1 tablespoon apricot jam and a pinch of ground cinnamon to the pan juices instead of the ginger marmalade in the above recipe. Soak 2 tablespoons finely chopped dried apricots and use these to garnish the dish instead of the julienne strips of orange rind.

Serves 4

Nutrition content per serving   Carbohydrate: 6g Fat: 13g
Fibre: 0g Kilocalories: 235

TOP: Monkfish Kebabs with Cumin & Mint; BOTTOM: Pork Medallions with Ginger.

TROUT FRIED WITH APPLES

The trout does not need a sauce, as the apples are moist and full of flavour.

4 large rainbow trout, cleaned
freshly ground black pepper
1 tablespoon lemon juice
4 rosemary sprigs
50g (2oz) butter
2 dessert apples, cored and thickly sliced
lemon slices, to garnish

Preparation time: 15 minutes
Cooking time: 12–14 minutes

1. Sprinkle the inside of the trout with plenty of pepper and the lemon juice and place a sprig of rosemary in the cavity. (Use a pinch of dried rosemary if the fresh herb is not available.)
2. Fry the trout in the butter over moderate heat for 6 minutes. Using wooden spatulas or fish slices, turn the fish over, taking care not to break the skin. Add the apples. Cook for a further 6–8 minutes, turning the apples once, until the fish are just cooked and the apples are deep golden brown. Transfer to a serving dish.
3. Serve the fish surrounded by the apples and garnished with twisted lemon slices.

Serves 4

Nutrition content per serving   Carbohydrate: 8g Fat: 21g
Fibre: 1g Kilocalories: 427

GRILLED LAMB STEAKS

1 × 1.5kg (3lb) leg of lamb, boned
salt
freshly ground black pepper
MAITRE D'HOTEL BUTTER:
50g (2oz) butter, softened
juice of ½ small lemon
1 tablespoon chopped fresh parsley

Preparation time: 15 minutes
Cooking time: 15–20 minutes

1. To make the maître d'hôtel butter, cream the ingredients together, and add salt and pepper. Shape into a roll, wrap and chill until firm.

FROM TOP TO BOTTOM: Trout Fried with Apples; Grilled Chicken with Warm Aïoli; Grilled Lamb Steaks.

2. Cut the lamb into steaks about 2.5cm (1 inch) thick. Trim off excess fat and rub both sides with salt and pepper.
3. Cook under a preheated hot grill, turning once. Like beef, lamb steaks are best left slightly pink in the centre. Serve hot, topped with a slice of maître d'hôtel butter.

Serves 4

Nutrition content per serving   Carbohydrate: 0g Fat: 30g
Fibre: 0g Kilocalories: 458

GRILLED CHICKEN WITH WARM AÏOLI

1 × 1.5kg (3lb) chicken, quartered, or 4 chicken
*   portions*
40g (1½oz) butter, melted
50g (2oz) plain flour
AIOLI (GARLIC MAYONNAISE):
2 egg yolks
salt
freshly ground pepper
15g (½oz) sugar
juice of 1 lemon
300ml (½ pint) oil (preferably olive)
3 garlic cloves, peeled and crushed
1 tablespoon boiling water

Preparation time: 10 minutes
Cooking time: 30–35 minutes

1. Brush the chicken with the melted butter, and dust with the flour. Cook under a preheated medium grill for about 15 minutes on each side or until brown and tender.
2. Meanwhile, beat the egg yolks with salt and pepper to taste, the sugar and the lemon juice in a heatproof bowl. Gradually add the oil in drops, beating all the time until the mayonnaise thickens. When half the oil has been added, the remainder may be added in a thin stream. Mix in the garlic and stabilize the sauce by beating in the boiling water. Taste and adjust the seasoning. Stand the bowl in hot water to heat through gently.
3. Arrange the chicken on a warmed serving dish and serve with the warm mayonnaise.

Serves 4

Nutrition content per serving   Carbohydrate: 15g Fat: 108g
Fibre: trace Kilocalories: 1186

HAM IN WINE CREAM SAUCE

450g (1lb) cooked ham or gammon, sliced
25g (1oz) butter
25g (1oz) plain flour
150ml ($\frac{1}{4}$ pint) milk
150ml ($\frac{1}{4}$ pint) dry white wine
1 tablespoon tomato purée
salt
white pepper
2–3 tablespoons grated Parmesan cheese

Preparation time: 15 minutes
Cooking time: 30 minutes
Oven: 200°C, 400°F, Gas Mark 6

1. Arrange the ham in an ovenproof dish.
2. Melt the butter in a pan, add the flour and cook for 1–2 minutes, stirring. Add the milk and bring to the boil, stirring all the time.
3. Add the wine and bring to the boil again, still stirring. Cook for 1–2 minutes, then stir in the tomato purée, salt and pepper. Pour over the ham and sprinkle the cheese on top.
4. Place in a preheated oven and cook for about 20 minutes until hot and browned on the top.

Serves 4

Nutrition content per serving   Carbohydrate: 7g Fat: 15g
Fibre: 0g Kilocalories: 333

BEEF TOURNEDOS DIJON

4 tournedos or fillet steaks, each weighing about
    150g (5oz), any barding fat removed
fresh ground black pepper
6 tablespoons Dijon mustard
50g (2oz) butter
4 tablespoons demerara sugar
4 tablespoons brandy
salt
fresh parsley sprig, to garnish

Preparation time: 5 minutes
Cooking time: 6–10 minutes

1. Sprinkle the steaks liberally on one side with pepper, then spread this side with one-third of the mustard. Melt the butter in a heavy-based frying pan and, when foaming, fry the steaks over brisk heat for 2 minutes, mustard side down. Spread the top side with half the remaining mustard, turn the steaks over and

cook for a further 2 minutes for rare, 3 minutes for medium, and 4 minutes for well-done steaks.
2. Remove the steaks with a slotted spoon and place on a sheet of foil over the grill rack. Spread one side of each steak with the remaining mustard, then sprinkle with the sugar. Put under a preheated hot grill for about 2 minutes until caramelized and bubbling.
3. Meanwhile, heat the brandy gently in a small pan, remove from the heat and ignite. When the flames have subsided, pour the brandy into the steak juices in the frying pan. Stir vigorously, and add salt and pepper to taste. Serve the steaks with the juices poured over and garnished with parsley sprigs.

Serves 4

Nutrition content per serving   Carbohydrate: 12g Fat: 18g
Fibre: 0g Kilocalories: 367

TURKEY MOZZARELLA

225g (8oz) boned turkey breast
salt
freshly ground black pepper
25g (1oz) plain flour
25g (1oz) butter
100g (4oz) button mushrooms, sliced
4 tablespoons chicken stock
75g (3oz) mozzarella cheese, sliced

Preparation time: 15 minutes
Cooking time: about 25 minutes

1. Beat the turkey flat and cut into 4–6 pieces. Season well with salt and pepper and coat evenly with the flour. Melt the butter in a frying pan and fry the turkey until golden brown all over and cooked through – about 15 minutes. Transfer to a shallow flameproof dish.
2. Fry the mushrooms in the pan for 3–4 minutes, then spoon over the turkey. Add the stock and salt and pepper to taste to the pan and boil until reduced by half. Pour over the turkey.
3. Lay the slices of cheese on top and put under a preheated moderate grill. Cook until the cheese is melted and lightly browned. Serve hot.

Serves 2

Nutrition content per serving   Carbohydrate: 11g Fat: 20g
Fibre: 2g Kilocalories: 365

FROM TOP TO BOTTOM: Beef Tournedos Dijon;
Ham in Wine Cream Sauce; Turkey Mozzarella.

SALMON STEAKS IN RED WINE

6 salmon steaks, about 2.5cm (1 inch) thick
100–150g (4–5oz) unsalted butter
6 shallots, peeled and finely chopped
small bunch fresh parsley, finely chopped
1 garlic clove, peeled and finely chopped
6 black peppercorns, crushed
salt
300ml ($\frac{1}{2}$ pint) red wine
parsley sprig, to garnish

Preparation time: 5 minutes
Cooking time: 15–20 minutes
Oven: 190°C, 375°F, Gas Mark 5

1. Rinse the salmon quickly in cold water, then pat dry.
2. Melt 50g (2oz) of the butter in a large flameproof dish into which the salmon will fit snugly. Add the shallots and sweat for 2 minutes.
3. Put in the salmon steaks and brown for 1 minute on each side over a high heat.
4. Sprinkle over the remaining ingredients, cover with a butter paper and cook in a preheated oven for 10–15 minutes until the steaks are just done.
5. Pour off the cooking juices into a small saucepan; keep the salmon warm. Cut the rest of the butter into small pieces and whisk into the pan, one at a time, beating until each piece is

absorbed. Stop when the sauce is smooth and glossy. Pour immediately over the salmon, garnish and serve.

Serves 6

Nutrition content per serving   Carbohydrate: 1g Fat: 34g
Fibre: 0.5g Kilocalories: 447

SCAMPI WITH BRANDY SAUCE

25g (1oz) butter
2 medium onions, peeled and chopped
1 garlic clove, peeled and chopped
450g (1lb) raw, shelled scampi, thawed if frozen
salt
freshly ground black pepper
3 tablespoons brandy
1 teaspoon grated orange rind
juice of 1 orange
1 teaspoon cornflour
120ml (4fl oz) plain unsweetened yogurt
100g (4oz) button mushrooms, thinly sliced
pinch of cayenne pepper
TO GARNISH:
orange slices
fresh dill sprigs

Preparation time: 15 minutes
Cooking time: 15 minutes

1. Heat 15g ($\frac{1}{2}$oz) of the butter in a frying pan and fry the onion and garlic over moderate heat for 2 minutes, stirring once or twice. Add the scampi, season with salt and pepper and fry for 3–4 minutes, stirring frequently. Pour on the brandy, shake the pan well and set light to it with a match. Tip the pan, taking great care, so that the spirit burns evenly.
2. Add the orange rind and orange juice. Stir the cornflour into the yogurt and stir into the pan. Taste the sauce, adjust the seasoning if necessary, and simmer for 4–5 minutes.
3. Melt the remaining butter in a small pan and stir-fry the mushrooms for 2 minutes.
4. Stir the mushrooms and cayenne into the scampi and serve, garnished with twisted orange slices and dill sprigs.

Serves 4

Nutrition content per serving   Carbohydrate: 8g Fat: 7g
Fibre: 2g Kilocalories: 212

LEFT: Salmon Steaks in Red Wine.
RIGHT: Scampi with Brandy Sauce.

Light meals

◆

& SNACKS

For those times when something quick and not too substantial is called for – at lunchtime, after school, before the cinema, and so on – you can find delicious ideas in this chapter.

Pasta can be used in many ways to make quick yet nutritious dishes. Here there's a simple dish of penne (diagonally-cut macaroni) dressed with a spicy mixture of black olives, capers, parsley and olive oil. There's also a macaroni and tuna fish casserole topped with tomato slices and crushed crisps.

Haddock fritters with a spicy batter will be very popular with those who like curry flavours, as will a chicken, fruit and nut salad with a curried mayonnaise dressing.

You will also find a pizza, a quiche cooked in a frying pan, lots of sandwiches, nutty beefburgers, a puffed-up rarebit, and a very special version of beans on toast.

Grilled Pitta Pockets (see recipe on page 48).

GRILLED PITTA POCKETS

4 pitta breads
100g (4oz) cooked lamb, finely shredded
50g (2oz) mushrooms, thinly sliced
1 small bunch spring onions, trimmed and chopped
2 lettuce leaves, shredded
2 tomatoes, skinned, seeded and chopped
4 black olives, stoned and sliced
2–3 tablespoons plain Greek yogurt
salt
freshly ground black pepper
75g (3oz) cheese, grated

Preparation time: 20 minutes
Cooking time: 5–6 minutes

1. Carefully cut a slit across the top of each pitta bread but not through to the base. Gently open out the bread pockets each side of the slit.
2. Mix the lamb with the mushrooms, onions, lettuce, tomatoes, olives, yogurt and salt and pepper to taste, blending well. Stuff the pitta pockets equally with the mixture and place on a grill rack. Sprinkle the cheese on top.
3. Place under a preheated moderate grill and cook for about 5–6 minutes until golden and bubbly. Serve at once.

Variation: The pitta pockets can also be filled with a West Indian mixture: 100g (4oz) cooked diced chicken mixed with 50g (2oz) finely chopped pineapple, 50g (2oz) finely chopped green pepper, 1 small sliced banana, 25g (1oz) toasted almonds, 2–3 tablespoons mayonnaise and salt and pepper to taste. Top with the cheese and grill as above.

Serves 4

Nutrition content per serving   Carbohydrate: 46g Fat: 14g
Fibre: 5g Kilocalories: 378

PEANUT BEEFBURGERS

40g (1½oz) salted peanuts
225g (8oz) lean minced beef
1 tablespoon chopped onion
salt
freshly ground black pepper
1 egg yolk
2 tablespoons oil
2 baps, split
2 tomatoes, sliced

Preparation time: 10 minutes
Cooking time: 5–10 minutes

1. Chop most of the peanuts, leaving a few for garnish. Combine the mince, onion, chopped peanuts and plenty of salt and pepper and bind together with the egg yolk. Divide in two and shape into flat round cakes.
2. Heat the oil in a frying pan and fry the burgers for about 5 minutes on each side or until lightly browned and cooked through. Serve in warmed baps, topped with sliced tomatoes and a few whole peanuts.

Serves 2

Nutrition content per serving   Carbohydrate: 34g Fat: 38g
Fibre: 4g Kilocalories: 609

TUNA SCONE PIZZA

SCONE BASE:
40g (1½oz) butter
175g (6oz) self-raising flour
1 teaspoon salt
3–4 tablespoons milk
TOPPING:
25g (1oz) butter
1 onion, peeled and sliced
1 × 200g (7oz) can tuna fish, drained and mashed
1 teaspoon dried basil
100g (4oz) Cheddar cheese, finely grated
2 tomatoes, sliced

Preparation time: 20 minutes
Cooking time: about 25 minutes
Oven: 220°C, 425°F, Gas Mark 7

1. For the scone base, rub the butter into the flour and salt. Bind together with milk. Roll lightly to a 20cm (8 inch) round and place on a greased baking sheet.
2. For the topping, melt the butter and fry the onion until soft. Spread over the scone base. Top the onion with the tuna fish. Mix the basil and cheese together and sprinkle over the fish. Top with the tomato slices.
3. Bake in a preheated oven for 15–20 minutes. Serve hot in wedges.

Serves 4

Nutrition content per serving   Carbohydrate: 36g Fat: 34g
Fibre: 2g Kilocalories: 531

TOP: Tuna Scone Pizza; BOTTOM: Peanut Beefburgers.

MACARONI & FISH CRISP

6 handfuls quick-cooking macaroni
salt
1½ tablespoons cornflour
450ml (¾ pint) milk
25g (1oz) butter
1 large bunch of parsley, finely chopped
2 × 175g (6oz) cans tuna fish, drained and flaked
freshly ground black pepper
3 tomatoes, sliced
1 small packet of plain crisps, crushed

Preparation time: 15 minutes
Cooking time: 30 minutes
Oven: 230°C, 450°F, Gas Mark 8

1. Cook the macaroni in boiling salted water until barely tender, according to packet directions. Drain, then return to the pan.
2. Mix the cornflour to a paste with a little of the milk. Heat the remaining milk and the butter in the pan with the macaroni, then gradually stir in the cornflour paste. Bring to the boil and cook until the sauce thickens, stirring constantly. Remove from the heat, then gently fold in the parsley, tuna, salt and pepper.
3. Pour the mixture into an ovenproof dish and smooth the top. Arrange the tomato slices around the edge, then sprinkle the crisps in the centre. Bake in a preheated oven for 15 minutes, then serve immediately.

Serves 4

Nutrition content per serving   Carbohydrate: 77g Fat: 32g
Fibre: 7g Kilocalories: 719

SKILLET QUICHE

175g (6oz) shortcrust pastry, thawed if frozen
3 eggs
300ml (½ pint) single cream
175g (6oz) Cheddar cheese, grated
salt
freshly ground black pepper
1–2 large tomatoes, sliced

Preparation time: 15 minutes
Cooking time: 10–15 minutes

1. Roll out the pastry fairly thinly and cut a circle 25cm (10 inches) in diameter. Line a non-stick frying pan with the pastry, pressing it up the sides well. Prick the base all over with a fork. Cook over a gentle heat for 3–4 minutes.
2. Meanwhile, beat the eggs with the cream, two thirds of the cheese, and salt and pepper to taste. Pour this into the pastry case, cover and continue to cook for a further 3–4 minutes.
3. Uncover the pan and top the quiche with the sliced tomato, then sprinkle over the remaining cheese. Put under a preheated hot grill until the filling is puffed and golden. Slide the quiche carefully out of the pan on to a plate to serve.

Serves 4

Nutrition content per serving   Carbohydrate: 25g Fat: 47g
Fibre: 2g Kilocalories: 598

EGG FU-YUNG

2 dried Chinese mushrooms, or 50g (2oz) fresh
    mushrooms
25g (1oz) cooked peeled prawns
25g (1oz) cooked ham
25g (1oz) bamboo shoots
2–3 water chestnuts
4 eggs, beaten
1 tablespoon cornflour
4 tablespoons water
1 teaspoon salt
1 tablespoon dry sherry
3 tablespoons oil
fresh coriander sprigs, to garnish

Preparation time: 15 minutes, plus soaking
Cooking time: 4–5 minutes

1. If using the dried mushrooms, soak in warm water for about 20 minutes, then squeeze dry and discard the hard stalks.
2. Finely chop the dried or fresh mushrooms, prawns, ham, bamboo shoots and water chestnuts. Mix together with the beaten eggs. Add the cornflour, water, salt and sherry to the egg mixture and stir.
3. Heat the oil in wok or frying pan until smoking, then pour in the egg mixture and scramble with a fork until the mixture sets. Serve hot, garnished with coriander.

Serves 4

Nutrition content per serving   Carbohydrate: 3g Fat: 17g
Fibre: 0g Kilocalories: 208

FROM TOP TO BOTTOM: Macaroni & Fish Crisp; Skillet Quiche; Egg Fu-Yung.

TRIPLE DECKERS

4 large soft round rolls topped with sesame seeds
75g (3oz) butter, softened
100g (4oz) cold roast beef, shredded
4 tablespoons mayonnaise
1–2 teaspoons creamed horseradish
1 tablespoon snipped fresh chives
4 lettuce leaves
100g (4oz) mature Cheddar cheese, thinly sliced
1 tomato, thinly sliced
2 tablespoons chunky brown pickle
1 medium leek, cleaned and very thinly sliced
1 teaspoon grated lemon rind
1 tablespoon seedless raisins

Preparation time: 25 minutes

1. Cut three horizontal slits in each roll but do not cut through the bread to the other side. Spread the bread layers with the butter.
2. Mix the beef with half of the mayonnaise, the horseradish and chives, blending well.
3. Place a lettuce leaf on the bottom layer of each roll and top with an equal quantity of the beef filling.
4. Fill the middle layer of the rolls with slices of cheese, slices of tomato and the pickle.
5. Mix the leek with the lemon rind, remaining mayonnaise and raisins, blending well. Use to fill the top layer of the rolls.

Serves 4

Nutrition content per serving   Carbohydrate: 36g Fat: 43g
Fibre: 3g Kilocalories: 602

HERBY SAUSAGE PATTIES

450g (1lb) pork sausagemeat
1 teaspoon mixed dried herbs
1 tablespoon Worcestershire sauce
salt
freshly ground black pepper
oil for frying
4 baps
softened butter, for spreading
prepared mustard
onion rings, to garnish (optional)

Preparation time: 10 minutes
Cooking time: about 10 minutes

1. Mix together the sausagemeat, mixed herbs,

Worcestershire sauce, and salt and pepper to taste. Form the mixture into four patties.
2. Heat a little oil in a frying pan. Add the patties and cook for 3–4 minutes on one side, then turn them and cook for a further 4–5 minutes until browned and cooked through.
3. Meanwhile, split the baps in half and toast the cut sides. Spread them with butter and a little mustard and serve each sausage patty between two bap halves, topped with onion rings, if liked.

Serves 4

Nutrition content per serving   Carbohydrate: 42g Fat: 53g
Fibre: 2g Kilocalories: 704

THOUSANDS ON A RAFT

25g (1oz) butter
1 medium onion, peeled and finely chopped
1 garlic clove, peeled and crushed
1 green pepper, cored, seeded and thinly sliced
1 × 400g (14oz) can kidney beans, drained
1 × 425g (15oz) can baked beans
4 tablespoons tomato ketchup
1 tablespoon Worcestershire sauce
½ teaspoon salt
1 teaspoon freshly ground black pepper
2 teaspoons mild chilli powder
175g (6oz) Cheddar cheese, grated
4 large slices of hot buttered toast

Preparation time: 15 minutes
Cooking time: 15 minutes

1. Melt the butter in a frying pan. Add the onion, garlic and green pepper and fry for 5 minutes or until the onion is soft. Stir in the kidney beans, baked beans with the can juice, ketchup, Worcestershire sauce, salt, pepper and chilli powder. Cook for a further 5 minutes, stirring from time to time.
2. Stir in the cheese and cook, stirring constantly, for 3 minutes or until melted.
3. Place the hot buttered toast on four warmed serving plates and spoon the bean mixture over them. Serve at once.

Serves 4

Nutrition content per serving   Carbohydrate: 47g Fat: 27g
Fibre: 13g Kilocalories: 519

FROM TOP TO BOTTOM: Triple Deckers; Herby Sausage Patties; Thousands on a Raft.

SPICY HADDOCK FRITTERS

1kg (2lb) haddock fillet, skinned
1 egg, size 1
300ml (½ pint) water
225g (8oz) plain flour
1–2 teaspoons curry powder
salt
freshly ground black pepper
oil for deep frying
175ml (6fl oz) thick mayonnaise
3 tablespoons plain unsweetened yogurt
¼ teaspoon ground turmeric
1 small green chilli, seeded and very finely chopped
TO GARNISH:
lemon slices
fresh coriander leaves

Preparation time: 15 minutes
Cooking time: 15–20 minutes

1. Cut the haddock into bite-sized cubes and dry between paper towels.
2. Whisk the egg until frothy, then beat in the water. Mix well until amalgamated, then gradually sift in the flour, whisking all the time to make a really smooth batter. Add the curry powder, and salt and pepper to taste and beat again.
3. Fill a deep fat fryer one-third full of oil and heat to a temperature of 190°C (375°F) or until a cube of stale bread turns golden in 50 seconds.
4. Add the fish cubes to the bowl of batter, turning them to coat completely.
5. Lower a few cubes into the hot oil and deep fry for 4–5 minutes or until golden and puffed. Lift out with a slotted spoon and drain on paper towels. Keep hot while the remaining fritters are fried.
6. Mix together the mayonnaise, yogurt, turmeric and chilli and put into a small bowl. Serve with the fritters, garnished with coriander leaves and lemon slices.

Serves 4

Nutrition content per serving   Carbohydrate: 46g Fat: 51g
Fibre: 2g Kilocalories: 839

CURRIED CHICKEN SALAD

For special occasions, serve this salad on bought plain or spiced poppadums.

350g (12oz) cooked chicken meat, skinned
2 bananas, peeled and sliced
1 tablespoon lemon juice
50g (2oz) shelled cashew nuts (salted or unsalted)
25g (1oz) raisins
50g (2oz) dried apricots, coarsely chopped
shavings of fresh coconut, toasted, to garnish
DRESSING:
3 tablespoons mayonnaise
1 tablespoon finely chopped onion
½ teaspoon hot Madras curry powder
½ teaspoon lemon juice
2 tablespoons grated sweet apple
1 teaspoon mango chutney
pinch of salt

Preparation time: 20 minutes, plus chilling

1. To make the dressing, mix the mayonnaise with the onion, curry powder, lemon juice, apple, chutney and salt, blending well.
2. Cut the chicken into bite-sized pieces. Place in a serving bowl with the bananas and lemon juice, tossing gently to mix. Add the cashew nuts, raisins and dried apricots, blending well.
3. Spoon the dressing over the salad ingredients and toss well to mix.
4. Chill lightly before serving, sprinkled with the toasted coconut.

Serves 4

Nutrition content per serving   Carbohydrate: 26g Fat: 21g
Fibre: 6g Kilocalories: 388

LEFT: Spicy Haddock Fritters.
RIGHT: Curried Chicken Salad.

SURPRISE LOAF

550g (1¼lb) cooked chicken meat
1 long French stick
6–10 lettuce leaves, washed and drained
softened butter, for spreading
225g (8oz) cooked ham, finely chopped
3 hard-boiled eggs, chopped
5 tablespoons light mayonnaise
3 tablespoons tomato ketchup
1 tablespoon lemon juice
salt
freshly ground black pepper

Preparation time: 25 minutes

1. Skin the chicken and chop into bite-sized pieces.
2. Cut the French loaf in half lengthways, and scoop out the bread from the bottom half, leaving just a thin layer all round. Make breadcrumbs with the scooped out bread and reserve for another recipe. Line the bottom half with the lettuce leaves.
3. Lightly spread the top half of the loaf with butter.
4. Put the chicken, ham and hard-boiled eggs in a bowl, add the mayonnaise and tomato ketchup and mix thoroughly.
5. Add the lemon juice, and salt and pepper to taste and mix again, then pile into the lettuce-lined bread, pressing in with the back of a spoon to level. Replace the top half of the loaf.
6. Cut across into slices to serve.

Serves 4–6

Nutrition content per serving   Carbohydrate: 32–21g
Fat: 37–24g Fibre: 2–1g Kilocalories: 670–447

FRENCH BREAD PIZZAS

1 large long French stick
3 tablespoons tomato purée
1 × 227g (8oz) can tomatoes, drained and chopped
1 teaspoon dried oregano or marjoram
salt
freshly ground black pepper
100g (4oz) Cheddar cheese, grated
2 × 50g (2oz) cans anchovy fillets in oil, drained
few black olives

Preparation time: 15 minutes
Cooking time: 12–14 minutes

1. Slice the French stick in half lengthways and then in half crossways, on a slant. Place under a preheated hot grill and toast the cut surfaces until golden.
2. Spread the cut surfaces with the tomato purée. Top with the tomatoes, herbs, salt and pepper to taste and cheese.
3. Arrange the anchovy fillets in a lattice over the cheese and garnish with the olives.
4. Place under a preheated moderate grill and cook for about 10 minutes until golden and bubbly.
5. Serve hot.

Variation: Use bacon and stuffed green olives instead of anchovies and black olives. Cook 225g (8oz) back bacon rashers under a preheated moderate grill until crisp. Cool then crumble the bacon coarsely. Sprinkle over the tomato base, top with the cheese and garnish with a few sliced stuffed olives. Cook as above.

Serves 4

Nutrition content per serving   Carbohydrate: 31g Fat: 13g
Fibre: 2g Kilocalories: 297

TOP: Surprise Loaf; BOTTOM: French Bread Pizzas.

SOUFFLED RAREBITS

25g (1oz) butter
1 tablespoon plain flour
150ml (¼ pint) Guinness
1 teaspoon prepared mustard
225g (8oz) mature cheese, grated
2 eggs, separated
salt
freshly ground black pepper
4 slices wholemeal bread
cayenne pepper

Preparation time: 10 minutes
Cooking time: 10 minutes

1. Melt the butter in a saucepan over a gentle heat. Stir in the flour and cook for 1 minute. Remove the pan from the heat and gradually stir in the Guinness. Bring to the boil gently, stirring until thickened. Add the mustard, grated cheese, egg yolks, and salt and pepper to taste, stirring well. Remove the pan from the heat.
2. Toast the slices of wholemeal bread on one side only.
3. Whisk the egg whites until they form stiff peaks, then fold them lightly but thoroughly into the cheese mixture. Spread a generous amount of the cheese mixture on the untoasted side of each piece of bread, making sure it reaches to the edges of the bread.
4. Put under a preheated moderately hot grill and cook until the cheese topping is golden and bubbling. Sprinkle each rarebit with a little cayenne, cut them in half diagonally and serve immediately.

Serves 4

Nutrition content per serving   Carbohydrate: 16g Fat: 28g
Fibre: 3g Kilocalories: 399

TOASTED CHICKEN, SWEETCORN & CELERY SANDWICH

2 large slices brown bread
softened butter, for spreading
50g (2oz) cooked chicken meat, chopped
2 tablespoons sweetcorn relish
1 tablespoon finely chopped celery
salt
freshly ground black pepper
celery leaves, to garnish (optional)

Preparation time: 5 minutes
Cooking time: 5 minutes

1. Spread both slices of bread thinly but evenly with butter.
2. Place one slice of bread, buttered side down, on the rack of the grill.
3. Mix the chicken with the sweetcorn relish, celery and salt and pepper to taste.
4. Spread the chicken mixture evenly over the slice of bread on the rack. Top with the other slice, buttered side uppermost. Press the slices of bread gently together.
5. Place the sandwich under a preheated moderately hot grill and cook for 4–5 minutes, turning the sandwich once. Serve immediately, garnished with celery leaves, if liked.

Makes 1

Nutrition content per serving   Carbohydrate: 39g Fat: 10g
Fibre: 6g Kilocalories: 363

TOP: Souffléd Rarebits; BOTTOM: Toasted Chicken, Sweetcorn & Celery Sandwich.

PENNE WITH SPICY OLIVE SAUCE

450g (1lb) penne (diagonally-cut macaroni)
salt
120ml (4fl oz) olive oil
½ teaspoon ground ginger
generous pinch of grated nutmeg
freshly ground black pepper
1 garlic clove, peeled and crushed
3 tablespoons capers
75g (3oz) stoned black olives, sliced
2 tablespoons chopped fresh parsley
fresh basil sprigs, to garnish

Preparation time: 3 minutes
Cooking time: 11–12 minutes

1. Cook the penne in boiling salted water for 10 minutes. Drain thoroughly.
2. Return the cooked penne to the pan, together with the oil, ginger, nutmeg, pepper, garlic, capers, olives and parsley. Stir over a gentle heat for 1–2 minutes. Serve immediately, garnished with basil sprigs.

Serves 4

Nutrition content per serving   Carbohydrate: 86g Fat: 28g
Fibre: 7g Kilocalories: 631

SCRAMBLED KIPPERS

50g (2oz) butter
2 spring onions or 1 shallot, peeled and chopped
4 eggs
2 tablespoons top of the milk
2 kippers, or 1 × 225g (8oz) packet of kipper fillets, poached and flaked
1 tablespoon chopped fresh parsley
salt
freshly ground black pepper
crisp crescents of fried bread, to garnish

Preparation time: 15 minutes
Cooking time: 8–10 minutes

1. Melt the butter in a saucepan, add the onion and soften over a low heat.
2. Beat the eggs lightly, just enough to break them up, then add the top of the milk, kipper flesh, parsley and salt and pepper to taste. Pour the mixture into the butter and onion and cook slowly until soft and creamy, stirring with a wooden spoon.
3. Serve on a hot dish garnished with crescents of fried bread.

Serves 4

Nutrition content per serving   Carbohydrate: trace Fat: 22g
Fibre: 0g Kilocalories: 287

CHEESE & BACON FRIZZLES

If your frying pan is not large enough to hold this amount of mixture all at once, then you will have to cook the frizzles in two batches.

1 large potato, peeled and grated
½ onion, peeled and very finely chopped
50g (2oz) Cheddar or Edam cheese, grated
4 back bacon rashers, rinds removed, finely chopped
4 tablespoons self-raising flour
1 egg, beaten
freshly ground black pepper
4 tablespoons vegetable oil

Preparation time: 15 minutes
Cooking time: 15 minutes

1. Put all the ingredients in a bowl, except the oil, and beat well.
2. Heat the oil in a large non-stick frying pan. Add the mixture to the pan in spoonfuls and fry for 7 minutes on each side until golden brown and crisp. Serve immediately.

Makes 8

Nutrition content per frizzle   Carbohydrate: 9g Fat: 16g
Fibre: 1g Kilocalories: 199

FROM TOP TO BOTTOM: Penne with Spicy Olive Sauce; Scrambled Kippers; Cheese & Bacon Frizzles.

Convenience

♦

FOODS

The cans, jars and packets kept in the well-stocked storecupboard can make meal preparation much easier for the busy cook. It is no wonder that these are called convenience foods.

The recipes in this chapter give some clever ideas for using canned fish – in a paste and a mousse, to be served as starters, and in a casserole topped with cheese and breadcrumbs. Canned soups are used as excellent instant sauces, as well as providing a good base for a very individual soup.

Packets of instant mashed potato are put to good use in a fish pie, in corned beef hash and surrounding poached eggs on a bed of baked beans.

Quick desserts can be put together using canned fruit. Here there's a fool made with gooseberries, canned custard and whipped cream, plus a black cherry compote flamed with brandy.

Plaice with Cucumber Sauce (see recipe on page 64).

PLAICE WITH CUCUMBER SAUCE

750g (1½lb) plaice fillets, skinned
75g (3oz) butter
2 tablespoons anchovy paste, or 3 tablespoons
  anchovy essence
1 small cucumber, diced
1 teaspoon chopped fresh dill
1 × 275g (10oz) can condensed mushroom soup
4 tablespoons plain unsweetened yogurt
1 tomato, skinned, seeded and chopped
salt
freshly ground black pepper
fresh dill sprig, to garnish

Preparation time: 10 minutes
Cooking time: 15 minutes

1. Rinse the fillets and dry them well. Melt the butter in a frying pan, add the anchovy paste or essence and fish fillets, then fry over a medium heat until the fish is golden, turning once only.
2. In a bowl combine the remaining ingredients with salt and pepper to taste and spoon over the fish. Cover the pan and heat through gently for about 5 minutes.
3. Remove the fillets to a warm serving dish and pour over the sauce. Garnish with dill.

Serves 4

Nutrition content per serving   Carbohydrate: 8g Fat: 27g
Fibre: trace Kilocalories: 424

CORNED BEEF HASH

1 × 100g (4oz) packet instant mashed potato mix
450ml (¾ pint) boiling water
50g (2oz) butter
¼ teaspoon mustard powder
freshly ground black pepper
1 × 350g (12oz) can corned beef, shredded
1 onion, peeled and finely chopped
chopped fresh parsley, to garnish

Preparation time: 15 minutes
Cooking time: about 25 minutes

1. Put the potato mix in a bowl, then gradually stir in the boiling water. Add half the butter, the mustard and plenty of pepper and beat well to mix. Fold in the corned beef.
2. Melt the remaining butter in a non-stick frying pan, add the onion and fry over gentle heat until soft. Add the potato mixture and fry over brisk heat for 10 minutes. Stir the mixture and turn it over occasionally, then flatten it into a cake shape with a spatula and smooth the top. Fry over moderate heat for 5 minutes or until golden brown underneath.
3. Invert a plate over the pan and turn the hash out on to the plate. Slide back into the pan and fry for a further 5 minutes or until golden brown on the underside. Cut into wedges, sprinkle with parsley and serve hot.

Serves 4

Nutrition content per serving   Carbohydrate: 20g Fat: 21g
Fibre: 4g Kilocalories: 367

EGGS IN A NEST

25g (1oz) butter
3 eggs
1 × 425g (15oz) can baked beans
1 × 100g (4oz) packet instant mashed potato mix
450ml (¾ pint) boiling water
salt
freshly ground black pepper
75g (3oz) Cheddar cheese, grated

Preparation time: 10 minutes
Cooking time: about 15 minutes

1. Heat water in the large shallow pan of an egg poacher. Put the egg poacher on the top and divide half of the butter equally between the poaching cups. Crack in the eggs, cover with a lid and poach over gentle heat for 5 minutes.
2. Meanwhile, put the baked beans in a separate pan and heat gently. Sprinkle the potato mix over the boiling water and beat until smooth. Add the remaining butter and salt and pepper to taste.
3. Spread the potato around the base and sides of a hot round flameproof dish, or individual ramekins, to make the nest, then pour the baked beans into the centre. Slide the eggs on top of the beans and sprinkle the cheese on top. Put under a hot grill for 5 minutes until the cheese melts.

Serves 3

Nutrition content per serving   Carbohydrate: 39g Fat: 22g
Fibre: 16g Kilocalories: 433

LEFT: Corned Beef Hash; RIGHT: Eggs in a Nest.

SALMON HERB MOUSSE

50g (2oz) curd cheese or Petit Suisse
1 tablespoon lemon juice
1 × 90g (3½oz) can salmon, drained and flaked
salt
freshly ground black pepper
chopped fresh chives, to garnish

Preparation time: 15 minutes

1. Blend the curd cheese or Petit Suisse with the lemon juice, and add the flaked salmon, salt and pepper.
2. Sprinkle chopped chives over the mousse and serve.

Serves 2

Nutrition content per serving   Carbohydrate: trace Fat: 10g
Fibre: 0g Kilocalories: 135

TOMATO CHOWDER

Sweet and spicy in flavour, this colourful chowder makes good use of canned foods.

1 × 275g (10oz) can condensed tomato soup,
   undiluted
450ml (¾ pint) milk
1 × 400g (14oz) can tomatoes, sieved
1 × 326g (11½oz) can sweetcorn, drained
1 tablespoon Worcestershire sauce
1 teaspoon sugar
freshly ground black pepper
100g (4oz) Cheddar cheese, grated, to finish

Preparation time: 10 minutes
Cooking time: 10 minutes

1. Combine all the ingredients with salt and pepper to taste in a large saucepan and bring slowly to the boil, stirring constantly. Pour into a hot serving bowl or individual bowls and sprinkle the top with the grated cheese.
2. Put under a preheated hot grill for 5 minutes or until the cheese melts and is bubbling. Serve immediately.

Serves 4–6

Nutrition content per serving   Carbohydrate: 32–21g
Fat: 18–12g Fibre: 5–4g Kilocalories: 343–228

FISH PIE MORNAY

25g (1oz) butter
450g (1lb) white fish fillets, skinned and cut into
   pieces
1 × 300ml (½ pint) packet cheese sauce mix
about 300ml (½ pint) milk
pinch of cayenne pepper
salt
freshly ground black pepper
100g (4oz) peeled cooked prawns
1 × 100g (4oz) packet instant mashed potato mix
450ml (¾ pint) boiling water
3 hard-boiled eggs, sliced

Preparation time: 10 minutes
Cooking time: about 30 minutes

1. Melt half the butter in a large shallow pan, add the white fish and fry over gentle heat until lightly coloured. Remove from the pan and drain off any excess liquid.
2. Mix the sauce mix with the milk according to packet directions, then pour into the pan. Bring to the boil, stirring occasionally, then lower the heat and cook until thick.
3. Return the fish to the pan, add the cayenne and salt and pepper to taste, and cook gently for 10 minutes. Add the prawns and cook for a further 5 minutes.
4. Make the potato mix with the water according to packet directions.
5. Arrange the eggs over the fish mixture, cover with the potato and mark with a fork. Dot with the remaining butter. Put under a hot grill to cook for 10 minutes until browned, turning the pan occasionally to ensure even browning. Serve hot.

Serves 4

Nutrition content per serving   Carbohydrate: 26g Fat: 23g
Fibre: 4g Kilocalories: 463

FROM TOP TO BOTTOM: Salmon Herb Mousse; Tomato Chowder; Fish Pie Mornay.

PEACH CONDE

$\frac{1}{2}$ teaspoon ground cinnamon
1 × 425g (15oz) can creamed rice
1 × 400g (14oz) can peach halves, drained
4 glacé cherries, quartered, to finish

Preparation time: 15 minutes, plus chilling

1. Stir the cinnamon into the rice.
2. Chop the peaches finely, reserving 8 slices for decoration.
3. Layer the rice and chopped peaches in four individual glasses, starting and ending with a layer of rice. Top with the reserved peach slices and decorate with quartered glacé cherries. Chill before serving.

Variation: You can vary the fruit, according to taste and availability.

Serves 4

Nutrition content per serving   Carbohydrate: 42g Fat: 3g
Fibre: 1g Kilocalories: 195

TUNA CHEESE WITH DILL

40g (1$\frac{1}{2}$oz) butter
1 medium onion, peeled and finely chopped
1 × 275g (10oz) can condensed cream of
    mushroom soup
large pinch of salt
$\frac{1}{2}$ teaspoon white pepper
1 teaspoon dried dill
1 × 275g (10oz) can tuna fish, drained and flaked
$\frac{1}{2}$ × 200g (7oz) can sweetcorn, drained
75g (3oz) Gruyère cheese, grated
6 thin slices of Gruyère cheese
40g (1$\frac{1}{2}$oz) fresh breadcrumbs

Preparation time: 15 minutes
Cooking time: 20 minutes

1. Melt the butter in a frying pan. Add the onion and fry for 5 minutes or until soft. Stir in the soup, salt, pepper and dill and bring to the boil. Stir in the tuna fish, sweetcorn and half the grated cheese. Cook, stirring occasionally, for about 3 minutes, or until heated through.
2. Transfer to a flameproof serving dish. Lay the cheese slices over the top.
3. Mix together the remaining grated cheese and the breadcrumbs. Sprinkle this mixture over the cheese slices to cover completely.
4. Place the dish under a preheated moderately hot grill and cook for 5–8 minutes or until the top is brown and bubbly. Serve at once.

Serves 4

Nutrition content per serving   Carbohydrate: 20g Fat: 39g
Fibre: 4g Kilocalories: 538

DEVILLED SARDINE PASTE

Canned sardines are curious creatures in that, like fine wines, they mature with age. There even used to be a club in London that met once a year to discuss the current 'vintage' and sample others from the 'cellar'. So keep a good stock and turn the cans over occasionally so the oil can blend with the fish. Always buy a good brand, preferably in olive oil, although some of the finest Portuguese sardines are now canned in other vegetable oil.

3 × 120g (4$\frac{1}{2}$oz) cans sardines, drained
up to 275g (10oz) unsalted butter, slightly
    softened
3–4 tablespoons lemon juice
salt
freshly ground black pepper
cayenne pepper, to taste
fresh parsley sprig, to garnish
hot toast, to serve

Preparation time: 5–15 minutes, plus chilling

1. Mash the sardines and 75g (3oz) butter to a coarse purée with a fork.
2. Add 3 tablespoons lemon juice, and salt and pepper to taste and mash again. Taste and add more butter if necessary; the texture must not be too dry. Adjust the seasoning if necessary, then mash in cayenne pepper to taste; the paste should be fairly spicy.
3. Spoon into small ramekins or other dishes and chill for at least 45 minutes.
4. Serve the sardine paste, chilled, garnished with parsley, and accompanied by hot toast.

Serves 6

Nutrition content per serving   Carbohydrate: 0g Fat: 40g
Fibre: 0g Kilocalories: 380

TOP RIGHT: Peach Condé; TOP LEFT: Tuna Cheese with Dill; BOTTOM: Devilled Sardine Paste.

GOOSEBERRY FOOL

1 × 400g (14oz) can gooseberries, drained
1 × 425g (15oz) can custard
1–2 drops almond essence
150ml (¼ pint) double cream, whipped
2–3 tablespoons toasted flaked almonds, to
*   decorate*

Preparation time: 15 minutes

1. Mash the gooseberries in a bowl with a potato masher. Add the custard and almond essence and stir well to mix.
2. Fold in the cream, then spoon into individual glasses and decorate each one with a sprinkling of flaked almonds.

Variation: Any canned fruit can be substituted for the gooseberries.

Serves 4

Nutrition content per serving   Carbohydrate: 31g Fat: 25g
Fibre: 3g Kilocalories: 364

CHERRIES JUBILEE

This dessert is supposed to have been created in the 1890s by a French chef who was celebrating his fiftieth birthday. It can be prepared at the table in a chafing dish, for a spectacular flaming presentation.

2 × 425g (15oz) cans black cherries
4 tablespoons redcurrant jelly
coarsely grated rind and juice of 1 orange
3 tablespoons brandy
fresh mint sprigs, to decorate
whipped cream or vanilla ice cream, to serve

Preparation time: 10 minutes
Cooking time: 5–8 minutes

1. Drain the cherries and put them into a bowl. Measure 6 tablespoons of the cherry juice and put into a shallow pan with the redcurrant jelly and orange rind and juice. Stir over a gentle heat until the jelly has melted.
2. Add the brandy and the cherries and bring quickly to the boil. Carefully set light to the surface of the juice, and shake the pan gently until the flames die down.
3. Spoon the cherry mixture into individual dishes and add a mint sprig to each serving. Serve immediately, with whipped cream. Alternatively, arrange scoops of vanilla ice cream in individual glass bowls and spoon over the cherry mixture. Serve immediately.

Serves 4

Nutrition content per serving   Carbohydrate: 45g Fat: 4g
Fibre: 1g Kilocalories: 237

LEFT: Gooseberry Fool.
RIGHT: Cherries Jubilee.

Desserts

◆

There is no doubt that perfectly ripe fresh fruit is the simplest dessert, but if you want to serve something a bit more special that doesn't take hours to prepare, you'll be delighted by the recipes in this chapter. Not one of them takes more than 30 minutes to make.

Hot desserts include a lemon-cream dipping sauce for cubes of gingerbread and brandy snaps, honey baked peaches, bananas fried and flamed with brandy, an easy soufflé omelette filled with warmed jam, and an ice cream sundae with a rich hot fudge sauce.

If you prefer a cold sweet, you'll find lots to choose from: a mousse flavoured with rum, chestnut and chocolate, and another made with marshmallows and coffee; fruit salads; the easiest frozen bombe imaginable; and soft cheese hearts flavoured with Cointreau.

Chocolate Waffles (see recipe on page 74).

CHOCOLATE WAFFLES

50g (2oz) plain chocolate, broken into pieces
4 tablespoons water
75g (3oz) unsalted butter
2 eggs
75–100g (3–3½oz) sugar
175g (6oz) plain flour
2 teaspoons baking powder
120ml (4fl oz) milk
75g (3oz) shelled walnuts, chopped
oil for greasing
TO SERVE:
chocolate ice cream or whipped cream
cherry sauce (optional)

Preparation time: 10 minutes
Cooking time: about 15 minutes

1. Stir the chocolate pieces and water together in a saucepan over a low heat, until the chocolate melts and the mixture forms a paste. Off the heat, beat in the butter, then the eggs and finally the sugar. Sift the flour and baking powder together on to a sheet of greaseproof paper and add alternately with the milk. Stir in the walnuts.
2. Pour a little batter into a hot oiled waffle iron. Bring the cover down and cook for 2–3 minutes on either side.
3. Serve the waffles hot with chocolate ice cream or whipped cream and cherry sauce, if liked.

Serves 6

Nutrition content per serving   Carbohydrate: 45g Fat: 27g
Fibre: 2g Kilocalories: 443

HOT SPICED PEACHES

4 large ripe fresh peaches
grated rind of 1 lemon
¼ teaspoon ground cinnamon
2 tablespoons clear honey
25g (1oz) butter
fresh mint sprigs, to decorate

Preparation time: 10 minutes
Cooking time: 15–20 minutes
Oven: 180°C, 350°F, Gas Mark 4

1. First skin the peaches. Dip them one at a time in boiling water and the skins will slide off

very easily. Cut each peach in half and twist to separate the halves, then remove the stone.
2. Arrange the peach halves cut side up in an ovenproof dish. Sprinkle with the lemon rind and cinnamon then spoon the honey over.
3. Place a dot of butter in the cavity of each peach, cover the dish and bake in a preheated oven for about 20 minutes until the peaches are tender and juicy. Serve hot, decorated with mint, with cream.

Serves 4

Nutrition content per serving   Carbohydrate: 15g Fat: 5g
Fibre: 1g Kilocalories: 105

LEMON FONDUE

600ml (1 pint) single cream
5 egg yolks
finely grated rind of 3 lemons
50g (2oz) caster sugar
cubes of gingerbread and/or brandy snaps, to serve

Preparation time: about 5 minutes
Cooking time: about 15 minutes

1. Heat the cream in the top of a double saucepan until tepid, or use a heatproof bowl over a pan of simmering water.
2. Put the egg yolks, lemon rind and caster sugar into a bowl and whisk until thick and creamy.
3. Pour the tepid cream on to the egg yolk mixture and whisk in.
4. Return the lemon mixture to the top of the double saucepan and cook, stirring, until the fondue mixture will coat the back of a wooden spoon.
5. Transfer the fondue to an ovenproof dish and place over a fondue pan of simmering water. Serve with gingerbread cubes and brandy snaps for dipping.

Serves 4–6

Nutrition content per serving   Carbohydrate: 18–12g
Fat: 41–28g Fibre: 0g Kilocalories: 473–315

TOP: Hot Spiced Peaches; BOTTOM: Lemon Fondue.

TROPICAL FRUIT SALAD

It is important that all the fruits are ripe. Mangoes should be yellow with a lot of red showing. Papayas should be yellow all over. Both mangoes and papayas should feel soft, and be fragrant. Guavas must have turned completely yellow and be soft to the touch. They have a very pungent smell and should be kept away from delicately flavoured foods. Buy the fruit several days before it is needed and store in a warm place until ripe.

1 ripe mango, peeled
1 ripe papaya, peeled
2 very ripe guavas, peeled and sliced
1 kiwi fruit, peeled and diced
3–4 slices fresh pineapple, peeled, cored and diced
1 star fruit, sliced (optional)
3 passion fruit (optional)
100g (4oz) small strawberries or large strawberries, halved (optional)
150–300ml ($\frac{1}{4}$–$\frac{1}{2}$ pint) orange juice
2–3 tablespoons rum (optional)
1–2 bananas

Preparation time: 20–30 minutes, plus chilling

1. Cut the mango flesh away from the long flat stone. Cut the papaya in half and remove the seeds. Cut both fruits into even dice.
2. Place the mango, papaya, sliced guavas and kiwi fruit in a bowl with the pineapple and star fruit, if using.
3. Cut the passion fruit in half. Scoop out the seeds and juice and add to the fruit. Add the strawberries, if using.
4. Pour over 150ml ($\frac{1}{4}$ pint) of the orange juice and the rum. Cover well and refrigerate.
5. Just before serving, peel and slice the bananas and add them to the fruit. Add more orange juice if necessary or if desired. Toss the fruit well so that the colours are well mixed.
6. Serve the fruit chilled, alone or accompanied by crisp biscuits and whipped cream or ice cream.

Serves 6–8

Nutrition content per serving   Carbohydrate: 36–27g Fat: trace
Fibre: 4–3g Kilocalories: 165–123

LEFT: Tropical Fruit Salad.
RIGHT: Bananas Flambé.

BANANAS FLAMBE

4 medium bananas, peeled and cut in half lengthways
50g (2oz) butter, melted
50g (2oz) light brown sugar
4 tablespoons brandy
flaked almonds, toasted, to decorate

Preparation time: 7–8 minutes

1. Fry the bananas in the melted butter until golden and just tender.
2. Sprinkle in the sugar and stir carefully to coat the fruit. Stir in the brandy.
3. Bring to the boil. Immediately set alight and serve sprinkled with a few flaked almonds.

Serves 4

Nutrition content per serving   Carbohydrate: 46g Fat: 14g
Fibre: 7g Kilocalories: 345

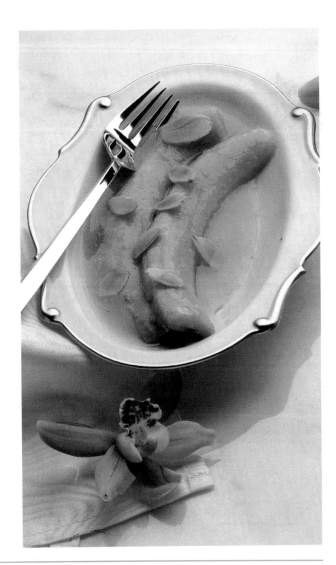

GINGER CREAMS

150ml (¼ pint) whipping cream, lightly whipped
300ml (½ pint) plain unsweetened yogurt
75g (3oz) ginger nut biscuits, finely crushed
25g (1oz) crystallized or stem ginger, chopped
TO SERVE:
pieces of crystallized or stem ginger
crisp biscuits

Preparation time: 15 minutes

1. Stir together the cream, yogurt and biscuits, then fold in the ginger.
2. Spoon into individual glasses. Top each serving with pieces of ginger and serve with biscuits.

Serves 6

Nutrition content per serving   Carbohydrate: 15g Fat: 11g
Fibre: trace Kilocalories: 171

ITALIAN CHEESE HEARTS

25g (1oz) caster sugar
100g (4oz) full fat soft cheese
1 tablespoon ground almonds
1 tablespoon Cointreau
TO DECORATE:
2 large strawberries, sliced
strawberry leaves, washed (optional)

Preparation time: 15 minutes

1. Beat the sugar with the cheese until the cheese is soft and creamy.
2. Gradually beat in the ground almonds, then the Cointreau, to make a soft consistency.
3. Spoon the mixture into the centre of two flat serving plates. Alternatively, press the mixture into a heart-shaped cutter on a plate. Lift off the cutter, leaving a decorative shape to the dessert.
4. Decorate with strawberry slices and leaves, if available.

Serves 2

Nutrition content per serving   Carbohydrate: 16g Fat: 26g
Fibre: 1g Kilocalories: 324

COFFEE & MARSHMALLOW MOUSSE

225g (8oz) marshmallows, halved
2 teaspoons instant coffee granules
100ml (3½fl oz) boiling water
2 egg whites
150ml (¼ pint) whipping cream, whipped to form soft peaks
40g (1½oz) shelled walnuts, chopped
TO DECORATE:
2–3 tablespoons whipped cream
chopped chocolate flakes

Preparation time: 20–25 minutes, plus chilling

1. Put the marshmallows in a large bowl and place over a pan of hot water. Dissolve the coffee in the 100ml (3½fl oz) boiling water, add to the marshmallows and leave until they have melted, stirring occasionally. Cool the mixture.
2. Place the mixture in a pan of ice water, or in the ice compartment of the refrigerator, to chill until almost set.
3. Whisk the egg whites until stiff. Gently fold the cream, nuts and, lastly, the egg whites into the marshmallow mixture. Pour into a serving bowl and leave until set.
4. Decorate with swirls of cream and chocolate flakes. Serve chilled.

Serves 6

Nutrition content per serving   Carbohydrate: 24g Fat: 12g
Fibre: trace Kilocalories: 214

FROM TOP TO BOTTOM: Ginger Creams; Coffee & Marshmallow Mousse; Italian Cheese Hearts.

APRICOT TOASTS

Bread, whether sweet or plain, dipped in a custard mixture and pan fried is known in France as Pain Perdu and England as Poor Knights of Windsor. In both countries the recipe dates back to medieval times. The dessert can be simply served sprinkled with sugar and topped with jam or cream or more sumptuously with brandied fruits. For a richer custard substitute cream for the milk.

1 egg
1 tablespoon milk
4–8 small slices fruited or plain bread, crusts
  removed
40g (1½oz) butter
2 tablespoons caster sugar
½ teaspoon ground cinnamon
1 × 275g (10oz) can apricot halves in juice,
  drained
whipped cream
1 tablespoon chopped pistachios or toasted almonds

Preparation time: 5 minutes
Cooking time: 5 minutes

1. Beat the egg and milk together and dip in the bread slices until coated on both sides and the egg mixture is absorbed.
2. Melt the butter and fry the slices of bread until crisp and golden on both sides. Drain on paper towels.
3. Mix the sugar and cinnamon together and sprinkle on to the bread. Top with the apricots, whipped cream and nuts. Serve at once.

Serves 4

Nutrition content per serving   Carbohydrate: 36g Fat: 14g
Fibre: 2g Kilocalories: 279

GINGER MERINGUE NESTS

6 tablespoons ginger marmalade
1 tablespoon undiluted orange squash
6 meringue nests
6 scoops of vanilla ice cream
fresh pouring cream, to serve

Preparation time: 15 minutes
Cooking time: 2–3 minutes

1. Put the marmalade and orange squash in a

pan and heat gently until melted, stirring occasionally. Leave to cool.
2. Put the meringues on individual serving plates, then put one scoop of ice cream in each. Pour the sauce over the ice cream, then serve immediately with fresh pouring cream handed separately.

Serves 6

Nutrition content per serving   Carbohydrate: 52g Fat: 4g
Fibre: trace Kilocalories: 244

TOFFEE APPLES

4 large, firm dessert apples, peeled and cored
4 tablespoons plain flour
1 tablespoon cornflour
2 egg whites
oil for deep-frying
100g (4oz) sugar
2 tablespoons water
1 tablespoon lard
1 tablespoon sesame seeds

Preparation time: 15 minutes
Cooking time: about 8 minutes

1. Cut each apple into eight pieces. Sprinkle the pieces with a little of the flour. Mix the remaining flour with the cornflour and egg whites to make a batter.
2. Heat the oil in a wok or saucepan. Coat each piece of apple with batter, and deep-fry for about 3 minutes. Remove the apple pieces with a slotted spoon and drain them thoroughly on paper towels.
3. Place the sugar and water in a saucepan and stir over a gentle heat. Add the lard, increase the heat and continue stirring until the sugar has caramelized.
4. Add the apple pieces, stir, and add the sesame seeds. Serve as soon as they are well blended.
5. Place a bowl of cold water on the table and dip each piece of apple into this to harden the toffee before eating.

Serves 4

Nutrition content per serving   Carbohydrate: 53g Fat: 13g
Fibre: 3g Kilocalories: 326

FROM TOP TO BOTTOM: Apricot Toasts; Toffee Apples; Ginger Meringue Nests.

LEMON SYLLABUB

This dish should be eaten the day it is prepared, otherwise it will separate.

150ml (¼ pint) white wine or sherry
75g (3oz) caster sugar
2 tablespoons lemon juice
2 teaspoons grated lemon rind
300ml (½ pint) whipping cream
julienne strips of lemon rind, to decorate

Preparation time: 10 minutes, plus infusing

1. Place the wine, sugar and lemon juice and rind in a basin. Leave to infuse for 1 hour.
2. Add the cream and whisk the mixture until it is stiff enough to stand in soft peaks, about 5 minutes with an electric hand whisk.
3. Spoon into individual glasses and decorate with lemon rind. Chill until required.

Serves 4–6

Nutrition content per serving Carbohydrate: 22–15g
Fat: 26–18g Fibre: 0g Kilocalories: 348–232

MELON & RASPBERRIES IN SAUTERNES

1 small ripe Galia melon
175g (6oz) fresh or thawed frozen raspberries
½ bottle Sauternes, chilled

Preparation time: 5 minutes, plus chilling

1. Halve the melon and either scoop out small balls using a melon baller or cut the flesh into small cubes.
2. Divide the melon and raspberries equally between four glass dishes. Pour over any melon juice, cover and chill in the refrigerator for at least 2 hours.
3. Just before serving, pour the chilled Sauternes into each dish to almost cover the fruit. Serve immediately.

Serves 4

Nutrition content per serving Carbohydrate: 7g Fat: 0g
Fibre: 4g Kilocalories: 90

CHESTNUT & CHOCOLATE MOUSSE

100g (4oz) plain chocolate
175g (6oz) canned chestnut purée
2 tablespoons dark rum
25g (1oz) icing sugar
150ml (¼ pint) double or whipping cream
a little plain chocolate, grated, to decorate

Preparation time: 15 minutes, plus chilling

1. Break the chocolate into pieces and put into a heatproof bowl placed over a saucepan of simmering water. Heat to melt the chocolate, stirring until smooth. Remove from the heat and allow to cool slightly.
2. Beat the chestnut purée until smooth. Mix in the rum and icing sugar. Stir in the chocolate until evenly blended.
3. Whip the cream until it just holds its shape. Fold into the chestnut mixture. Divide between four dessert dishes and chill until ready to serve.
4. Decorate with grated chocolate.

Serves 4

Nutrition content per serving Carbohydrate: 29g Fat: 25g
Fibre: 0g Kilocalories: 362

FROM TOP TO BOTTOM: Lemon Syllabub; Chestnut & Chocolate Mousse; Melon & Raspberries in Sauternes.

CHOCOLATE FUDGE

50g (2oz) butter, plus extra for greasing
100g (4oz) plain chocolate, broken into pieces
5 tablespoons evaporated milk
1 teaspoon vanilla essence
450g (1lb) icing sugar, sifted
50g (2oz) chopped nuts, toasted (optional)
100g (4oz) plain chocolate, broken into pieces, to
  decorate

Preparation time: 15 minutes, plus cooling
Cooking time: about 5 minutes

1. Grease an 18–20cm (7–8 inch) square tin with butter.
2. Place the butter, chocolate and evaporated milk in a small heatproof bowl set over a pan of hot water. Stir vigorously until smooth. Add the vanilla essence.
3. Pour the chocolate mixture into the icing sugar and nuts, if using. Beat until blended.
4. Press into the greased tin and leave in a cool place to set.
5. When cool, melt the chocolate for decoration in a heatproof bowl set over a bowl of hot water. Stir until smooth. Spread over the fudge with a spatula. Roughen the surface with a fork and leave until set.
6. Cut the fudge into squares. Store in an airtight container for 3–4 days.

Variations: Use milk or white chocolate for a milder chocolate flavour, and replace the nuts with an equal quantity of chopped glacé cherries and chopped angelica.

Makes 50–60 pieces

Nutrition content per piece   Carbohydrate: 12–10g Fat: 3–2g
Fibre: trace Kilocalories: 72–60

PEARS POACHED IN MARSALA

2–3 firm ripe pears
25g (1oz) butter
3 tablespoons Marsala
3 tablespoons orange juice
2 tablespoons double cream
fresh mint sprig, to decorate

FROM TOP TO BOTTOM: Chocolate Fudge; Pears
Poached in Marsala; Soufflé Omelette.

Preparation time: 10 minutes
Cooking time: 15–20 minutes

1. Peel and quarter the pears, then remove the cores. Melt the butter in a pan, add the pears and cook gently for about 5 minutes, until the pears are well coated and beginning to soften.
2. Add the Marsala and orange juice to the pan and simmer for 10–15 minutes, until the pears are tender.
3. Remove the pan from the heat and stir in the cream. Serve warm, decorated with mint.

Serves 2

Nutrition content per serving   Carbohydrate: 22g Fat: 18g
Fibre: 4g Kilocalories: 266

SOUFFLE OMELETTE

For 4 people, double the ingredients and work with 2 pans or use 1 larger pan.

3 eggs, separated
1–2 tablespoons water
2 teaspoons caster sugar
25g (1oz) unsalted butter
2–3 tablespoons jam, warmed
a little icing sugar

Preparation time: 5–10 minutes
Cooking time: 5–7 minutes

1. Beat the egg yolks and 1 tablespoon of water with the sugar. Whisk the egg whites until they stand in stiff peaks and fold into the yolks.
2. Heat the butter in a 15–18cm (6–7 inch) frying pan. Take care not to let it colour. When it stops frothing, pour in the egg mixture and cook for 2–3 minutes until golden brown on the underside.
3. Place under a preheated grill for 2–3 minutes until set and golden brown on top.
4. Meanwhile, heat the jam in a small pan, adding a teaspoon or two of water if necessary.
5. When the omelette is cooked, slide it out on to a hot serving dish and make a light cut through the surface of the omelette (this makes it easier to fold). Pour the jam into the centre of the omelette, fold the top half over and sift a little icing sugar over the top. Serve at once.

Serves 2

Nutrition content per serving   Carbohydrate: 10g Fat: 18g
Fibre: 0g Kilocalories: 240

HOT FUDGE SUNDAE

vanilla or other flavoured ice cream
whipped cream
toasted flaked almonds or chopped walnuts
FUDGE SAUCE:
75g (3oz) butter
1 tablespoon golden syrup
75g (3oz) brown sugar
4 tablespoons evaporated milk

Preparation time: 10–15 minutes
Cooking time: 10 minutes

1. Place all the ingredients for the sauce in a heavy-based pan and heat gently until the sugar has dissolved, stirring all the time with a wooden spoon. Bring to the boil, then remove the pan from the heat.
2. Put scoops of ice cream into four individual serving dishes. Spoon over the hot sauce and top with whipped cream and chopped nuts. Serve immediately.

Serves 4

Nutrition content per serving   Carbohydrate: 39g Fat: 29g
Fibre: 0g Kilocalories: 428

SNOW QUEEN

300ml (½ pint) double cream
2 tablespoons brandy
1 tablespoon caster sugar
100g (4oz) meringue shells, roughly broken
fresh mint sprig, to decorate (optional)
raspberries or sweetened raspberry purée, to serve

Preparation time: 15 minutes, plus freezing and thawing

1. Whip the cream until stiff and stir in the brandy and caster sugar. Fold in the meringue.
2. Spoon the mixture into a lightly oiled 600ml (1 pint) pudding basin or bombe mould and press in gently so there are no air pockets. Cover, seal and freeze.
3. Unwrap, unmould on to a serving dish and thaw for 15 minutes in the refrigerator. Decorate with a mint sprig and raspberries or serve with a sweetened raspberry purée.

Serves 4

Nutrition content per serving   Carbohydrate: 28g Fat: 36g
Fibre: 0g Kilocalories: 457

BAKED ALASKA

100g (4oz) trifle sponges
2 tablespoons sweet sherry
3 egg whites
150g (5oz) caster sugar
600ml (1 pint) vanilla ice cream

Preparation time: 25 minutes
Cooking time: 4–5 minutes
Oven: 220°C, 425°F, Gas Mark 7

1. Halve the trifle sponges and use them to line a shallow ovenproof serving dish. Moisten the sponges with the sherry.
2. Whisk the egg whites until stiff. Gradually whisk in half the sugar and continue whisking for 1 minute, then fold in the remaining sugar.
3. Pile the ice cream on to the sponges, leaving a 1cm (½ inch) border round the edge. Spread the meringue over the ice cream and sponges to cover completely, swirling the meringue to make a decorative effect.
4. Place the dish on a baking sheet and bake in a preheated oven for 4–5 minutes or until the meringue is lightly browned and crisp. Serve immediately.

Serves 6

Nutrition content per serving   Carbohydrate: 60g Fat: 8g
Fibre: trace Kilocalories: 328

LEFT: Hot Fudge Sundae (top); Snow Queen (bottom).
ABOVE: Baked Alaska.

Teatime

◆

TREATS

Home-made cakes and biscuits are always more delicious than those you have bought, but often there just isn't any time to bake. If that's the problem at your house, then you'll welcome the teatime recipes in this chapter.

Crushed digestive biscuits are a short-cut base for many toothsome treats. Here they are mixed with melted chocolate, sultanas, glacé cherries and orange rind to make biscuit squares, as well as combined with fruit, nuts, marshmallows and sherry for a loaf cake.

Muesli squares made from porridge oats, coconut, sesame seeds and nuts are very popular with children, as are cornflake-based Crispy Crackles. In addition, there are recipes for drop scones, American-style muffins, flapjacks and quick scones.

Honeyed Drop Scones (see recipe on page 90).

HONEYED DROP SCONES

225g (8oz) self-raising flour
½ teaspoon ground cinnamon
50g (2oz) caster sugar
1 tablespoon clear honey
1 egg, beaten
300ml (½ pint) milk
oil for cooking

Preparation time: about 8 minutes
Cooking time: 15–20 minutes

1. Sift the flour, cinnamon and sugar into a mixing bowl. Mix the honey and egg together and pour into the centre of the flour. Gradually beat in the milk until smooth.
2. Lightly grease a heavy-based frying pan, or griddle, and heat until moderately hot. Drop tablespoons of the mixture on to the pan or griddle, well spaced apart, and cook until bubbles appear on the surface and the underside is golden brown. Turn over and cook the other side until golden brown.
3. Remove the scones from the pan and wrap in a tea towel to keep warm. Continue making scones until all the batter is used.
4. Serve warm, spread with butter or cream cheese, and more honey, if wished.

Variations: Flavour with ground mixed spice or 1 teaspoon finely grated lemon rind instead of cinnamon.

Makes 18–20
Nutrition content per scone   Carbohydrate: 14–13g Fat: 3–2g
Fibre: trace Kilocalories: 83–75

FRUIT & NUT CAKE

225g (8oz) digestive biscuits, coarsely crumbled
175g (6oz) candied peel, chopped
175g (6oz) glacé cherries, chopped
100g (4oz) raisins
100g (4oz) shelled Brazil nuts, chopped
1 teaspoon ground mixed spice
75g (3oz) marshmallows, chopped
3 tablespoons sherry
3 tablespoons black treacle
100g (4oz) plain chocolate, broken into pieces
TO DECORATE:
shelled Brazil nuts
glacé cherries, halved

Preparation time: 20 minutes, plus chilling
Cooking time: 5 minutes

1. Lightly grease a 1kg (2lb) loaf tin and line with greased greaseproof paper.
2. Mix the crumbled biscuits with the peel, cherries, raisins, nuts and mixed spice.
3. Place the marshmallows, sherry, black treacle and chocolate in a bowl. Stand the bowl over a saucepan of gently simmering water and stir until all the ingredients have melted.
4. Stir the melted ingredients into the biscuit and fruit mixture, and mix thoroughly together.
5. Pour into the prepared loaf tin and spread the surface level. Cover with a piece of greased greaseproof paper. Chill until the cake is quite firm. Turn out and decorate with Brazil nuts and glacé cherries. Slice to serve.

Makes one 1kg (2lb) cake (18 slices)
Nutrition content per slice   Carbohydrate: 31g Fat: 8g
Fibre: 2g Kilocalories: 198

CHOCOLATE BISCUIT SQUARES

175g (6oz) plain chocolate
50g (2oz) butter
225g (8oz) digestive biscuits
grated rind of 1 orange
100g (4oz) sultanas
50g (2oz) glacé cherries, chopped
icing sugar, sifted, to decorate

Preparation time: 15–20 minutes, plus chilling

1. Melt the chocolate and butter in a heatproof bowl over a pan of hot water. Remove from the heat.
2. Put the biscuits in a polythene bag and crush with a rolling pin. Add to the chocolate mixture with the orange rind, sultanas and chopped cherries. Mix well and press into an 18cm (7 inch) square tin. Mark into 9 squares.
3. Chill well before cutting into squares. Sprinkle with a little icing sugar before serving.

Makes 9
Nutrition content per square   Carbohydrate: 42g Fat: 15g
Fibre: 2g Kilocalories: 310

TOP: Fruit & Nut Cake; BOTTOM: Chocolate Biscuit Squares.

MUESLI SQUARES

3 tablespoons honey
100g (4oz) butter
50g (2oz) soft light brown sugar
50g (2oz) chopped mixed nuts
100g (4oz) porridge oats
25g (1oz) desiccated coconut
50g (2oz) sesame seeds
100g (4oz) plain chocolate, melted (optional)

Preparation time: 10 minutes
Cooking time: 20 minutes
Oven: 180°C, 350°F, Gas Mark 4

1. Place the honey, butter and sugar in a saucepan. Heat gently until the butter has melted and the sugar has dissolved.
2. Stir in the nuts, oats, coconut and sesame seeds.
3. Press evenly into a greased 28 × 18cm (11 × 7 inch) shallow oblong tin. Bake in a preheated oven for 20 minutes, until golden brown.
4. Cool for 5 minutes in the tin, then cut into squares. Leave in the tin to cool completely. Dip one side of each square in the melted chocolate, if using.

Makes 18

Nutrition content per square   Carbohydrate: 13g Fat: 10g
Fibre: 1g Kilocalories: 150

TREACLE & SULTANA FLAPJACKS

150g (5oz) butter
75g (3oz) Barbados or molasses sugar
1–2 tablespoons black molasses
50g (2oz) sultanas
225g (8oz) jumbo or rolled oats
grated rind and juice of ½ lemon

Preparation time: 10 minutes
Cooking time: 40 minutes
Oven: 160°C, 325°F, Gas Mark 3

1. Melt the butter in a saucepan. Stir in the sugar and molasses. Add the sultanas, oats and lemon rind and juice and mix well. Press into a greased 25 × 20cm (10 × 8 inch) tin.

2. Bake in a preheated oven for 40 minutes. Allow to cool for 10 minutes, then cut into bars. Leave in the tin until completely cold.

Makes 12

Nutrition content per flapjack   Carbohydrate: 25g Fat: 12g
Fibre: 2g Kilocalories: 209

WELSH CAKES

225g (8oz) plain flour
1 teaspoon baking powder
¼ teaspoon ground mixed spice
50g (2oz) each butter and lard
75g (3oz) caster sugar
50g (2oz) currants
1 egg, beaten
2–3 tablespoons milk
oil for cooking

Preparation time: 20 minutes
Cooking time: about 8 minutes

1. Sift the flour, baking powder and spice into a mixing bowl. Cut the fats into the flour and rub in to make a breadcrumb consistency. Mix in the sugar and currants. Add the egg and enough milk to bind to a stiff dough.
2. Roll out the dough on a floured surface to 5mm (¼ inch) thick. Cut out 7.5cm (3 inch) rounds with a plain cutter.
3. Cook on a hot oiled griddle for 4 minutes on each side or until golden. Serve hot or cold.

Makes 8

Nutrition content per cake   Carbohydrate: 37g Fat: 13g
Fibre: 1g Kilocalories: 267

LEFT: Treacle & Sultana Flapjacks on the left; Muesli Squares on the right. RIGHT: Welsh Cakes.

AMERICAN BRAN MUFFINS

Unlike traditional British muffins, American muffins are deep and have a cake-like texture. Bake them in bun tins or in individual paper cases.

4 tablespoons oil
75g (3oz) soft dark brown sugar
75g (3oz) golden syrup
2 eggs, beaten
250ml (8fl oz) milk
50g (2oz) bran
75g (3oz) raisins
100g (4oz) self-raising flour
1 teaspoon baking powder
½ teaspoon bicarbonate of soda
½ teaspoon salt

Preparation time: 10 minutes
Cooking time: 15 minutes
Oven: 200°C, 400°F, Gas Mark 6

1. Place the oil, sugar, syrup, beaten eggs and milk in a large bowl. Mix thoroughly with a fork.
2. Add the bran and raisins and sift in the flour, baking powder, bicarbonate of soda and salt. Stir very lightly until the ingredients are just mixed.
3. Spoon the mixture into paper cake cases or greased bun tins until two-thirds full.
4. Bake in a preheated oven for 15 minutes, until well risen and firm to the touch. Serve warm, split in half and buttered.

Makes 20

Nutrition content per muffin   Carbohydrate: 15g Fat: 4g
Fibre: 2g Kilocalories: 100

CRISPY CRACKLES

50g (2oz) butter
2 tablespoons golden syrup
50g (2oz) drinking chocolate powder, sifted
50g (2oz) cornflakes

Preparation time: 10 minutes, plus cooling
Cooking time: 3 minutes

1. Melt the butter and golden syrup over a low heat. Remove from the heat and stir in the drinking chocolate and cornflakes, mixing well so the cornflakes are well coated in the chocolate syrup mixture.
2. Spoon into paper cases, set on a baking sheet, and leave to cool. They will set on cooling.

Makes 16

Nutrition content per crackle   Carbohydrate: 6g Fat: 3g
Fibre: trace Kilocalories: 52

QUICK SCONES

Using soft margarine enables all the ingredients for the dough to be added together, so that the scones are quickly prepared.

225g (8oz) self-raising flour
1 teaspoon baking powder
50g (2oz) soft margarine
25g (1oz) caster sugar
150ml (¼ pint) milk
milk, to glaze

Preparation time: 10 minutes
Cooking time: 12–15 minutes
Oven: 220°C, 425°F, Gas Mark 7

1. Sift the flour and baking powder into a bowl. Add the margarine, sugar and milk and mix to a soft dough.
2. Place on a floured surface and knead lightly. Roll out to a 1cm (½ inch) thickness and cut into rounds with a 6cm (2½ inch) fluted pastry cutter.
3. Place the scones on a greased baking sheet and glaze with milk. Bake in a preheated oven for 12–15 minutes, until well risen and golden brown. Serve warm, split and buttered.

Makes 10

Nutrition content per scone   Carbohydrate: 21g Fat: 5g
Fibre: 1g Kilocalories: 133

TOP LEFT: American Bran Muffins; TOP RIGHT: Crispy Crackles; BOTTOM: Quick Scones.

INDEX